Survivors

&

Partners

*Healing
the Relationships
of
Sexual Abuse Survivors*

PAUL A. HANSEN, Ph.D.

HERON HILL PUBLISHING CO. • LONGMONT, CO

Workshops and Lectures

Paul Hansen Ph.D. offers lectures and seminars on "Incest Survivors in Intimate Relationships" and "Healing the Relationships of Incest Survivors and Their Partners." He and his wife, Mimi Farrelly, offer workshops: "Healing the Wounds of Abuse for Couples" for survivors and their partners and for therapists working with such couples. If you are interested in bringing a workshop to your area or in attending workshops scheduled, please write to us at:

7548 Cresthill Drive, Longmont, CO 80501

This book is designed to provide information in regard to the subject matter covered. It is sold with the understanding that the publisher and author are not engaged in providing psychological or professional services through this medium. If such professional advice or service is required, the services of a competent professional should be sought. The purpose of this manual is to educate, inform and enlighten those persons who may have experienced the trauma of childhood sexual abuse and their partners, or who may be working with such individuals professionally. The author and Heron Hill Publishing shall have neither liability nor responsibility to any person or entity with respect to any loss or damage caused, or alleged to be caused, directly or indirectly by the information contained in this book.

Library of Congress Cataloging-in-Publication Data

Hansen, Paul A.,
   Survivors and Partners: healing the relationships of survivors of child sexual abuse.

   Bibliography: p.
   1. Incest victims—United States. 2. Partners of Incest Victims—United States. 3. Incest Victims—United States—Psychology 4. Adult Child Sexual Abuse—Psychology I. 5. Marriage Relationships. Title

ISBN 0-9629960-4-7

Printed in the United States of America

10 9 8 7 6 5 4 3 2 1   91-073755

Table of Contents

Acknowledgments

First and foremost, I want to acknowledge my wife, Mimi Farrelly, without whom this book would not have been written. She has been not only my fellow journeyer through this difficult experience but a support along the way and in addition provided copy editing which was invaluable. Many others read early versions of the book and provided helpful suggestions, copy editing and encouragement, including Clyde Reid, Bruce Fisher, Claudia Previn, Katie Klinger, and Trish Caetano. Barbara Ciletti provided the editorial expertise to help polish the manuscript for its final form. I also want to acknowledge the many women and men, individuals and couples who have been participants in our "HEALING THE WOUNDS OF ABUSE" workshops, who shared with us their pain, their fears, and their hopes, as well as their statements which spice the text of this book. Central in my learning about this subject have been the many courageous clients who have chosen to work with me in therapy as they set out to heal their painful wounds of sexual abuse. They have been my profound teachers. Lastly, I want to acknowledge my daughter Jori, who seemed somehow to understand at her tender age of 4 & 5, when her daddy was at his desk in front of the computer, to come in with hugs of encouragement and then allow him to continue.

Cover design: *Barbara J. Ciletti*
Typography: *Claudia (CPR) Previn*
Production: *Johnson Printing Company, Boulder, CO*

Disclaimer

This book is designed to provide information in regard to the subject matter covered. It is sold with the understanding that the publisher and author are not engaged in providing psychological or professional services through this medium. If such professional advice or service is required, the services of a competent professional should be sought. The purpose of this manual is to educate, inform and enlighten those persons who may have experienced the trauma of childhood sexual abuse and their partners, or who may be working with such individuals professionally. The author and Heron Hill Publishing shall have neither liability nor responsibility to any person or entity with respect to any loss or damage caused, or alleged to be caused, directly or indirectly by the information contained in this book.

Introduction

The information you are about to read is authentic. The material comes from my own experience as a partner of a sexual abuse survivor, from the experience of those who have been participants in our workshop: "HEALING THE WOUNDS OF ABUSE FOR COUPLES," (see Appendix 7) and from the experiences of those courageous people who have been my clients in psychotherapy as they have worked and fought to heal the wounds of their early childhood sexual abuse. I have not edited the client's and participant's quotations. They include the expletives they used to express their pain. This is a book for and about real people . . . all of us who are survivors and partners.

In 1987 my wife Mimi and I began conducting workshops on Healing the Wounds of Abuse for Couples (see appendices for more information) in which one of the partners was abused sexually or physically as a child. We were both personally and professionally well acquainted with the effects of child abuse and held a sincere desire to utilize our own learning in support of other couples who needed to triumph over past wounds. We decided we wanted to share the growth and learning we had achieved. The couples who have participated have found this to be enormously helpful. Just surviving as a couple these days is a real triumph in and of itself! As far as we could ascertain, no one else out there was doing this kind of work. In addition, despite a variety of treatment options for survivors, relatively little was being offered for a the survivor's primary partner or for their relationships.

Although the primary participants in our workshops have been couples, we also have had a few people come alone, some of whom are therapists. Some participants fit into both categories, being survivors or partners, and are also therapists who treat sexual abuse. Both my wife and I fit into that classification. She is an art therapist working with adults and children. I am a psychotherapist working primarily with adults.

The irony of all this is that in mid-1989 at age 52, in the midst of writing of this book, I made the shocking discovery that I too am a survivor of sexual abuse. I now have a much deeper and more authentic understanding of the kinds of feelings that the survivor goes through in the healing process. It has been sobering for my wife to find herself from time to time now in those double-binds that all partners experience, forced to shift from the role of survivor to partner.

I have chosen to use the term "survivor" rather than "victim" to identify the person who was sexually abused. As Laura Davis says in her book, *Courage to Heal*, "You have already survived the worst part, the abuse itself." I think it is important for both the survivor and the partner to begin to identify with this term, for it is a term of empowerment and advocacy. See yourselves as survivors. You have had your own holocaust. You are survivors.

I have written primarily from the perspective of the survivor being the female in the relationship and the partner being male. (Thus I have written the material using "she" for the survivor and "he" for the partner, rather than the more cumbersome "she/he"approach.) The most common experience for couples in our culture is that of the female survivor with a male partner. However we are also realizing that many men, as I have so painfully learned, were sexually abused as children as well. Whether male or female, the effects of abuse on a relationship are not substantially different. If you are the male survivor or female partner, I trust you can make that translation as you read.

Since I sometimes use the term partner to refer to the female survivor in the relationship, I will endeavor to capitalize the word "Partner" when I am referring to the **Partner of the survivor**. For readers who are in a relationship where both members are of the same gender, the terms survivor and Partner will be helpful. Gay and lesbian couples in our workshops have found that the effects of abuse on their relationships are essentially the same as those experienced by heterosexual couples.

I have included parts of our own personal story in this book. Although we feel publicly vulnerable in sharing our story, we do it hoping it will help you with your healing. We are not proud of our wounds, but we are proud of the healing process, as individuals and as a couple. This material has been printed in italics for easy comprehension. This book is written to provide you with hope and encouragement, whether you are in the process of healing your own wounds of abuse, or helping others to heal. Good luck!

Paul A Hansen PhD.

July 1991

1

ACCEPTING THE JOURNEY

*

"I am claiming my power to succeed, to be visible, to look sensuous in public, to be beautiful and not hide or throw up!"
A WOMAN SURVIVOR.

One of the most profound transformations possible in the human arena of growth can take place with the survivor of incest. This is the two-stage shift in consciousness, moving from being a victim to being a survivor, and then from survivor to thriver. What does this mean? And, how does such growth affect the survivor's primary relationship?

When a perpetrator forces a child into sexual experiences that are inappropriate for him or her, that child is a victim in every sense of the word. The child seldom experiences the power needed to say no, to resist the perpetrator, and to consequently affect the course of her life. To make sense of what is happening to her, to anchor her experience in a reasonable world, she may begin to make mental alterations of her view of reality. For instance, she may begin to believe that she deserves the abuse. She may believe that she is bad, and that her experience is some sort of punishment for something she has done wrong (a classic belief of the victim state). In some of the most severe cases of sexual abuse, she may develop alternate personalities in an effort to survive the experience (multiple personality disorder). This allows the abuse to happen to another person entirely hidden from her conscious awareness. Such a radical adaptive mechanism is more common when the sexual abuse is especially severe or connected with satanic or other abuse occurring in cultic or ritualized situations. Multiple personality disorder is a drastic extension of the common phenomenon of dissociation, or going numb that is experienced during the abuse and at other times by a large percentage of survivors.

HOW TO RECOGNIZE THE VICTIM

A victim, according to Webster, is someone injured or otherwise harmed by some act or circumstance outside their control. When persons are victimized as children, their view of themselves is profoundly affected and often creates a victim personality. In this state of consciousness the person often continues to feel powerless, and expects exploitation from the world. If this personality orientation is carried on into adult life, the victim still experiences herself at risk and powerless to affect what happens in her life. Things both good and bad, just seem to happen to her and she feels she can't do anything about them. She may complain, blame others or retreat into depression. Life will seem constantly painful for her. Somehow other people in the world may sense it too, and actually take advantage of her and her powerlessness. This only confirms her victimhood. She may act out these phenomena in her relationships, where she may be battered or repeatedly loved and left. It can also occur in her business and financial life, so that she seems constantly to get a raw deal, or be taken advantage of financially. She becomes another member of the walking wounded.

UNDERSTANDING THE SURVIVOR

A survivor is someone who is significantly different from a victim. Hear how one survivor puts it:

"I am, thank God, a *survivor*; I am no longer a
victim. No longer in hiding!"

I find it useful to think about the healing as a progression from
victim to survivor to thriver, and that each of these stages repre-
sents a change in an entire state of consciousness. Being a survivor is an intermediate state of consciousness. A survivor is not
willing to submit to abuse or to being taken advantage of anymore. She is no longer willing to be victimized.

"Surrender? Never!!"

She is starting to get up and fight for herself. She does not wear
a scarlet "V" on her clothing anymore. And yet she may find herself at a disadvantage in many personal, social, and business situations. She may be carrying lots of rage or fear. She has made a
commitment to heal from the abuse; she is determined not to let it
ruin or control her life any longer, but she still has a considerable
work to do in her healing process. She is still in substantial pain.
She may not have a good love relationship, or she may be in a relationship that is not yet as satisfying as she wants it to be, and she
is working to improve it. She has made a choice to grow, such as
this woman did:

"I can't believe how this has MADE me grow. It
was either that or die!"

BECOMING THE THRIVER

What does it really mean to be a thriver? A thriver is one who
flourishes, grows vigorously, and is able to live a successful life.
She operates with greater freedom and is able to create true mutu-
ality in a healthy relationship. In this stage the sexual abuse has
begun to fade into the background. It may never be forgotten totally, but it no longer negatively influences the thriver's every day
life. There is a deep acceptance of the abuse in a way that puts it
into perspective and gives the person power over the abuse instead

of the abuse having power over her life. Listen to what one thriver said:

> "I feel like I belong on the planet now, feeling connected to my body again through physical exercise and good health. I can say no, setting limits on work, on touching, on sex, etc. I feel like I have my life! I have creativity, joy, love and intimacy. And it's okay not to be perfect and to have more things to work out."

Thriving does not mean that problems or adversities no longer appear. It has to do with an attitude and a determination to succeed. This attitude, coupled with a sense of personal power over one's life, enables the thriver to feel successful at many, if not most of her life's endeavors.

WHEN WILL THE TURMOIL END?

A common experience for both the survivor and the Partner is the seemingly never-ending aspect of the emotional turmoil associated with healing of sexual abuse wounds. It is like riding on an endless roller coaster. It seems never to slow down and stop long enough for you to get off safely. Or if it does, it lulls you into thinking it is over, when suddenly it takes off again, up and down. So there you are, screaming in pain, anger, and resentment at having to go through all this stuff again!

When will it end, you ask? Will it ever end? These questions and the feeling of frustration behind them, are natural and normal for the survivor and the Partner. Each person, each couple will experience a different time table for healing. There is no set time frame for the healing from the abuse. As a therapist working with individuals and couples who are healing from sexual abuse, I've seen clients work from a minimum of 6 months up to a maximum of 3 years on their healing process. I want to assure you that it does heal. Yes, it will end! There is hope!

However, I believe that most survivors may find themselves in healing episodes periodically throughout their lives. Their experience is very similar to survivors of the Nazi holocaust of WW II and to Viet Nam veterans. Survivors of sexual abuse also experience Post Traumatic Stress syndrome. The scars of those wounds may always be there, and the effects of those wounds may come up intermittently, affecting your personal life and your relationships. But it need not negatively affect you every day of your life. I want to encourage you with the knowledge that each episode of the healing process gets a little easier and a little briefer. For the Partner or the survivor, it will be useful to keep the perspective that no matter how bad it is right now, this level of pain will not go on forever.

As a Partner, I clearly recall that very painful period in our lives which began nine years ago. I remember thinking: "I can survive this if I can just know it is going to end some day, that it is not going to go on forever. Maybe I can take it for six months, one year, or even two years. I have a strong personality, but I don't think I can handle this if I don't have an end in sight. So I asked my wife (an absurd question to expect her to answer), "How long is this going to go on?" And of course she could not give me a satisfactory answer. Happily, I can report that it did not go on forever, though it did last more than six months, and I did survive it! We survived it as a couple, and in the process built an even stronger marriage. We have just celebrated our eleventh wedding anniversary! It was and is worth it all!

HOW HEALING AFFECTS THE PARTNER AND THE RELATIONSHIP

How do these shifts in states of consciousness affect the Partner? How do they impact the relationship? For the Partner who has made taking care of the survivor and her upsets a second vocation or a primary focus in his life, the survivor's evolution into a thriver drastically upsets the balance in his life and in their relationship. You might think that the Partner would be thrilled to have a thriver in the house. He even may have been asking, praying and hoping for her to get to this stage of healing, to get through all her stuff. But if the relationship was formed on the basis of the Partner being the strong one and the survivor the needy, "sick" one, he is in for a rude awakening. Resentment sometimes occurs because a partner feels safer when his or her spouse is sick or weak. An emotionally healthy and successful thriver may well threaten the Partner. He may feel un-needed and unwanted. And it's true! He is not needed in the same way he was before healing. One Partner said:

> "I was there for you when you needed me. Why can't you be there for me now?"

She is out working and functioning well in the world, a happy, successful person! The subtle message is: why can't you still be weak and need me like you did previously. The Partner may become angry that the Survivor is well now.

Partners sometimes hold a secret fear that once the survivor is healed, she will no longer need him and will leave the relationship. He fears that she will go on to form a new relationship with someone else and he will be left feeling that he gave all his energy for nothing, that he went through all that pain for nothing. It could come true if he does not also shift his thinking to accept this "new" person and a new relationship. He may be angry at having to change too.

I have encountered Partners who have not been able to make that shift who end up divorced from that survivor, only to find themselves once again in a relationship with another survivor at some later date. They met and formed a relationship with another person who turned out to be a survivor. They seem to need someone to take care of and thus unconsciously find a sexually abused woman to fill that role.

The Partner who does not make the shift with his survivor partner may subtly (or not so subtly) try to pull the survivor back into the former needy, dependent state. Such manipulation may be consciously or unconsciously carried out by:

- opposing her desire to go back to work or upgrade her education or go to school,

- expressing resentment at the broader circle of friends and activities she now enjoys, while refusing to take the necessary risks to enrich his own life,
- not taking care of his own needs,
- putting her down, belittling her successes,
- controlling money available for therapy or for new clothes,
- controlling how they use their leisure time, and acting reluctant to try new experiences and activities.

I have seen all the above behaviors in our work with couples and individuals. The Partner needs to become an advocate for the growth of the survivor. It is a difficult and challenging role and one whose rewards may be hard to see initially and demanding to carry out over the long healing period. The needs of the Partner himself cannot be ignored either. Sometimes they are as great as those of the survivor, though for different reasons. Two needy people often find it hard to give each other what is needed. A useful attitude for the Partner to adopt is to be willing to see this situation as an opportunity for his own growth. Perhaps regard it as having an open ticket to becoming anything you want to become. See it as a grand opportunity for transformation and new life.

So, just as you have to mourn the death of the old ego states, you both may have to let go of the old relationship, the old marriage, and build a new one based on a new foundation of *mutual* strength, responsibility and capacities for love. Say goodbye to the old relationship based on one needy person and one caretaker, one giver and one receiver. I *do not* mean to say that you must end your relationship, divorce, or lose each other. Not at all! You can now have a new, richer, and far happier relationship than ever before.

ACCEPTANCE: AN ESSENTIAL FOR HEALING

In her classic work, *On Death and Dying*, Dr. Elizabeth Kubler Ross's describes acceptance as the fifth and final stage of preparation for death. (The first four are denial and isolation, anger, bargaining, and depression.) There are several parallels between dealing with a terminal illness and dealing with sexual abuse. Acceptance is a critical element in both cases. Dr. Bruce Fisher, in his book on divorce (*When Your Relationship Ends*), describes acceptance as the first stage of healing from divorce. Acceptance likewise plays a crucial role in healing from sexual abuse. I see three levels of acceptance which seem to correspond to the evolution through the three states of consciousness associated with healing: victim, survivor and thriver.

In the beginning stages of healing I see the first level of acceptance as accepting that the abuse really happened. Acknowledging that the abuse really occurred is particularly difficult when the abuse was rendered by a parent. Survivors easily think that they must have made up these memories of abuse, that it is not real. If you are a survivor, you may recognize this tendency. Not accepting its reality negates the healing process, and cancels the potential for healing. Hear the power of acceptance in this statement by a survivor.

> "I accept that it really happened. I accept that I was deceived, lied to, conned, and hurt. I don't accept evil as being part of me or part of those I choose to be near now. I choose and accept goodness to be in my life."

Another survivor says:

> "If I could accept it, then maybe I could love myself and others."

This statement gives us a clue to the next level of acceptance. The second level goes far beyond accepting the abuse as fact. At this level, the survivor and Partner accept that the abuse has had a profound impact on her life, her personality, their relationship, her relationship to the world and to herself. It has affected her career, her dreams of the future, and her Partner. As the survivor begins to fight her way free from the pervasive influence of the abuse, accepting the significance of that influence provides the first step toward achieving power over it. Notice the autonomy and strength in this survivor's assertion.

> "Acceptance gives me the right to set limitations with my father and to accept that no man or woman has the right to tell me when, how, or what I can do with my body. I own it! No one else does. Acceptance gives me power over "IT." I am no longer a victim."

The third level seems to be more difficult to articulate as well as to achieve. It involves accepting yourself as a whole person, and requires you to acknowledge that you are not a bad person. It demands a release of the guilt and shame from within you. It challenges you to see your potential for a happy marriage or relationship. You are called to accept new, more positive attitudes about yourself and the new life skills you have attained. A significant measure of spiritual peace accompanies this level of acceptance. You find peace within yourself. You can live in the moment and begin to embrace a more self-nurturing approach to your life. By doing so, you let go of the smaller vision of who you are, and thereby reduce the opportunities for self sabotage.

A loss of a sense of your personal identity comes with the shock of discovering abuse. Here, at this level of healing, the survivor-thriver is called to reclaim her identity, or rather to claim her true identity.

My wife Mimi makes a wonderful statement about her experience that I want to share here.

> *"When you are amnesic about your abuse, you believe you should be able to have what everyone else in your world has, but your actions seem to produce just the opposite and you end up in a downward spiral of self-defeat and shame. Then when you find out about the sexual abuse you*

enter a cycle of despair and rage you must work through in order to heal. You realize that you don't have everything that other people have. As you do the healing work you acquire a tool kit of attitudes and skills that enables you to be a happier, stronger person. Through this healing work I have learned things, different attitudes and skills, that help me in every part of my life. I've learned to discard what is useless and fight my way out of my self-imposed limitations. Also, I now know that if I can get through this horrible stuff, there is nothing I can't get through in life!"

One of our workshop participants describes it this way:

"Acceptance gives me freedom to be me, to become whatever I choose to be."

My earnest wish for you is that you all, survivors and Partners alike, become thrivers, and that your relationship thrives as well. The following chapters will, hopefully, clarify the journey toward health and peace and encourage you to take that journey. You may find it useful to turn to the Appendices 5 and 6 to understand more about the journey.

2

INTO
THE
WOODS!

✳

*"I must be losing my mind. Nothing makes
sense. I don't know who I am or
where I belong!"*

In the Broadway musical "Into The Woods," Steven Sondheim
weaves three or four well-known fairy tales together and creates
a delightful musical show. Listening closely to the lyrics and the
lines of the play allows one to catch some of the poignancy and
focus of Sondheim's intent. The theme conveys that each of us
must go "into the woods" to find ourselves. The characters are not
always pleased with what they discover about themselves there.
And while this is true in life for most people, it is particularly true
for those who begin to explore, and subsequently discover, the devastating memories of childhood sexual abuse. This particular set of
woods is very frightening. Sadly, the survivor cannot go into those
woods without taking her closest friend, partner, lover, or husband
with her. So if one person in a relationship decides to engage in the
exploration and healing, the other one is bound to be affected, even
dragged kicking and screaming into the whole tornadic phenomenon. In truth, the Partner finds himself already involved without having known it.

Like Dorothy in the *Wizard of Oz* (she is caught up in a Kansas tornado and lands in a totally different land), the couple caught up in this particular "tornado" will find themselves in a different "land," or more to the point, a different kind of relationship experience. When the storm subsides, their relationship, like Dorothy's life after her trip to Oz, will be transformed. And it should be a whole lot better.

HOW IT ALL BEGAN FOR US

Our story of dealing with the wounds of childhood sexual abuse begins before we got married. My wife and I had been dating for about six weeks and our romance was blossoming. Suddenly she announced that she would spend her three month summer teacher's vacation 3,000 miles away. This came as quite a blow to me. With this loss on top of a recent divorce, I decided not to date for a while and to deal with my grief.

At the end of the summer she returned and initiated contact. We resumed dating and after six weeks she again ended the relationship. And so the pattern continued, with several painful endings and beginnings. We were not to discover the root cause for this on-and-off behavior (sexual abuse as a child) for another three years, long after we were married.

The irony of dealing with sexual abuse in relationships is that it often seems to take a strong healthy relationship to provide a supportive enough environment for the survivor to allow the abuse to surface. Relationships which are not strong don't provide a safe climate, and the abuse remains in the unconscious. The effects may be there but it is likely there will be no awareness of abuse. So if you are beginning to acknowledge old wounds, compliment yourselves on the quality and strength of your primary relationship. It is a positive affirmation of your relationship.

BEFORE DISCOVERY:
WHAT'S HAPPENING TO US?

Much confusion accompanies the onset of the discovery of childhood sexual abuse. Your relationship may have begun like many others. You met, found yourself attracted, became friends, began dating, fell in love, became lovers, etc. Those times were filled with great excitement and romance. You had found the most wonderful partner, lover, friend. You seemed so well suited to each other.

Then things began to get serious. You occasionally discussed that "M" word, marriage. Or perhaps you talked of moving in together. You were in love! It was wonderful! Though occasionally there were those strange moments, which neither of you quite understood. The survivor had some unusual reactions during sex, such as going numb, withdrawing emotionally, or even having mental flashes that she was in bed with someone other than her lover or Partner. She may have directed bursts of rage at the Partner for little or no apparent reason.

While these reactions were disturbing, the overriding tenor of the relationship was one of joy and love for both of you. So you discounted those times as a fluke, as something that would get better or disappear. By doing so, you denied their significance. You moved ahead with your relationship, perhaps moving in together or getting married.

Typically, couples enter a honeymoon phase in the beginning of their relationship. Great joy, peace, companionship and harmony characterize this period. Eventually all couples pass through this phase and into another, deeper phase of their relationship. The honeymoon phase may last days, months or even years. During this time, couples concentrate on the success of the relationship and tend to ignore "problems" or possible negative factors. But such factors eventually develop to a level where they cannot be ignored. This is true for most couples and is especially true when one partner is a survivor of child sexual abuse. Such a time is especially confusing for the Partner.

When problems arise, it is easy for the Partner to blame himself for the problems. If you are the Partner, you will probably try harder to make the relationship work; or you may begin to blame your spouse for the problems that you encounter. Since survivors tend to feel more threatened as the relationship deepens, abuse-masking behaviors may intensify and make the relationship more difficult (see Chapter 5). The survivor may experience significant personality changes. You both may begin to ask: "What is happening to us?" The next step is usually for each to ask: "What's wrong with me?"

THE PARTNER'S VIEW

We constantly live in our own internal emotional reality. It is just like breathing. (And while we may or may not be aware of ourselves, we are always utilizing our internal reality, our beliefs and expectations, to process the events and experiences of our external world.) Partners are in a special place, as a result of the unexpected and unexplainable turmoil occurring in their relationship. If you are a Partner, you may find yourself saying some things similar to these quotes from other Partners:

> "What is happening? Sometimes in the middle of lovemaking she freezes and says: "Get off, you feel like my father!"

> "Why is it that every time we start to feel really happy and good with each other, she does something to sabotage the whole mood or relationship? Yet she often seems to blame me. Maybe there IS something wrong with me."

> "Who is this person that I married? She seems like a totally different person now than she did when we first got together."

> "I am feeling so rejected! I don't need this kind of pain."

> "I sometimes don't know what is real and what is not real. I get accused of things I never did or even thought, and yet it seems so real to her."

"One of us must be crazy! This relationship is
crazy. Why am I staying in this? I must be crazy
for staying in this kind of hell. Can we never get
back to a peaceful loving relationship? Is it always going to be this way, full of turmoil and
anxiety?"

The Partner, who is, at this stage, usually unaware of the childhood sexual abuse, has a difficulty making any sense of what is
happening to him. He frequently feels lonely, isolated, and rejected. It seems as if there is no one else in his world going through
what he is experiencing. If the commitment to the survivor or the
relationship is not very strong, he may begin counter rejecting.
This may take the form of denying interest in sex, having periods
of anger and rage, and cutting off communication. He will often
feel that his needs for companionship, love, understanding and sex
are not getting met in the relationship. If this perception is acute
enough, he may start reaching out to other women to meet his
needs, engage in affairs, or leave the relationship entirely. Once the
survivor begins to observe her partner's behavior, her self-esteem
undergoes further erosion, and the relationship suffers additional
damage. Her own healing process may be delayed or even pre-
vented; because the one thing that has provoked the release of the
survivor's behavior, could well squelched it. And, that one thing is
the relationship.

THE SURVIVOR'S VIEW

In the midst of turmoil like this, survivors ask: "What is happening to me? Am I going crazy?" "Is there something wrong with
me?" "Why am I in this incredible push-pull with my partner?"

This IS an equally confusing time for you, the survivor. You are
experiencing the most unusual and bizarre feelings you have ever
known. Just when you were getting what you believed you wanted
(a relationship with a person who loves you, and is emotionally

supportive and caring), you push it all away. Now you sometimes you want to end it, to get out. Sometimes the relationship feels "all wrong." You may have bursts of rage that seem to come out of nowhere. And, you didn't even know you could get that angry.) You may experience mood swings; alternating from feeling incredibly high and happy to feeling implausibly depressed. Your personal boundaries seem threatened. You begin to feel crowded, and develop a greater desire for more personal space. You may feel like you have to compete with your living partner for space. Its "my space versus your space." You may feel there is no room for you (in the closet, the bed, the house, etc.).

It is not uncommon for survivors to engage in compulsive behaviors. If you have been a substance abuser, you are more likely to have episodes of drinking or use of drugs. If you have used food as your "drug of choice," you are more likely to overeat, to have episodes of binge/vomiting (bulimia) or other bulimic behaviors (laxative purging etc.), or to withhold eating (anorexia). You may find yourself suddenly becoming fat, even obese, as if to make yourself sexually unattractive. Other compulsions may center on cleanliness. You may have sudden storms of house cleaning, feel constantly dirty and have to wash your hands all the time, take multiple showers, or brush your teeth every few hours.

THE COUPLE'S DILEMMA

As a couple you may honestly find yourselves questioning the wisdom of your choice to come together and the wisdom of your remaining together. "Are we just not meant to be together?" "Is our chemistry bad? Maybe we should just split or get divorced. When two people love each other deeply, they may really be confused about what they should do.

All couples go through a honeymoon phase when life seems wonderful and promising. But the honeymoon eventually ends and people move on in their life. People are continually challenged with the disillusionment that usually sets in after the honeymoon, not just survivors and their partners. Marriage or long term commitments provide the context for individuals to go "into the woods" to discover themselves. Many of you reading this book made the choice to be with each other before you knew what those woods contained, before you knew your relationship would have to deal with this kind of trauma. Some of you had some awareness of the abuse at the time you entered the relationship so your choice was not quite so blind. Either way it can be disillusioning and discouraging. Working with abuse in a relationship is no picnic. Choosing to read this book indicates that you either have some awareness now of abuse or that you suspect it. I believe that it will give you more information and understanding about the journey towards true self-discovery.

Your life lies before you. Do you choose to stay together or to go your separate ways? Do you choose to remain the way you are or do you choose to grow, to explore the very depths of your being, and allow a transformation to occur that is greater than you had ever imagined? When you honestly confront the issues and engage in the healing work to be done, your relationship can get better, perhaps better than you have envisioned. Chapter 3 discusses more of how couples are affected by this journey.

3

DISCOVERING
THE
ABUSE

✳

*"My first baby and I had
the same daddy!"*

or most couples, the time of discovery is certainly not a time
of calm, but rather one of tumult and upset. Some say: "Discovery is nauseating. I feel sick and I feel very small." I
know that discovery was upsetting for us. I think I felt almost as
much a shock as my wife did. For some it is a relief. "Discovery is
like a light at the end of the tunnel." "Now I have a reason for all
that anger." It can help to break the isolation and alienation felt by
survivors. As one woman said: "I will never forget the first time I
heard the word incest and realized I wasn't the only woman with
an awful past!"

For us, even though it was a relief to have some understanding of the source of the upsets in our lives, the disturbances continued unabated. At that time (1982) there was little or nothing in
the media or in print about sexual abuse. Sexual abuse had not yet
begun to show up in my psychotherapy practice. I think in those
days many of us in the profession were not wise enough to ask the
questions that would even discern if sexual abuse had occurred for
our clients.

FEAR OF THE UNKNOWN

During the period when sexual abuse memories are emerging, fear arises about what will arise next. One woman said: "I don't want any more memories to come. I've had enough!" The survivor fears the memories rising to the surface, as well as the possibility of what terrible things might still be hidden. However, survivors can also become quite driven, almost possessed, with trying to uncover just what happened. Hypnosis, body work, expressive therapies, and breath work can sometimes help but do not guarantee finding all the memories. When the traumatic experiences of childhood sexual abuse have been buried in the psyche for many years, the unconscious mind does not release them easily. It takes time for the survivor's unconscious to build a relationship of trust with the remembering conscious mind. If the survivor is strong enough, and handles the first memories well, more will come. If not, further memories can remain buried, though frustratingly near enough to the surface to let the survivor know they are there.

TRUST BECOMES A MAJOR ISSUE

During this period all the foundations of a survivor's trust are severely shaken. When coupled with the childhood feelings of fear that emerge, this questioning causes all persons and relationships to be scrutinized. When that foundation of trust between parent and child is broken, it severely affects the future ability of the person to be able to trust. The inner child of the survivor cries out: "If you can't trust a parent, who can you trust?" Sometimes there is such disbelief that a parent would so violate that trust relationship, that the survivor would rather question the memory than question the trust. They say: "How could my mother let this happen? or "How could a mother do this to her son (a male survivor)?"

Needless to say, such uncertainty causes great disruption in a marriage or adult love relationship.

WHO AM I?

Discovery is a time of shock, rage, disbelief, relief, sadness, and great confusion. "I'm losing my mind! Nothing makes sense. I don't know where I belong or who I am." Confusion rapidly becomes the common denominator for the days of discovery. The shock resulting from the discovery of incest or sexual abuse is so great, that it seems to throw the survivor's (and her Partner's) understanding of herself and her world, into total chaos, causing her to ask: "Who am I?" "It's such a shock . . .not me too!" With the revelation of this new aspect of her history, it seems as if all the basic foundations of life, her understanding of her self, her very identity, are now called into question.

She has changed! The very core of her internal reality seems to have shifted . . .and with it her identity. The Partner has difficulty understanding that his spouse/partner is, at some deep levels, not the same person anymore. She is not and cannot go on being the same person she used to be. When the known structure of one's life suddenly crumbles, it takes time to pick up the pieces and reassemble them in a new order. The survivor needs time to recover and reclaim those aspects of strength that have sustained her during the years of her life.

The non-survivor (eg. the Partner) has difficulty comprehending the depth of chaos created by the discovery of abuse. Basic responses to life and to people come into question. For most survivors it is like having your own private "holocaust," your own private hell. Few of us would demand that a survivor of the Nazi holocaust forget that it ever happened. Though we might tire of hearing about it and ask them to talk less about it, we could not humanely ask them to forget it or ignore that it ever happened. The same is true for the survivor of sexual abuse.

If one of the individuals in a relationship changes this profoundly, we can see that the relationship itself must change. When this occurs Partners may feel bewildered and sometimes ask themselves:

> "What happened to the person I married? This is not the person I fell in love with. What do I do now?"

> "I wonder if I will ever get my partner back!"

Hopefully, their dismay will not lead to a hasty decision to end the relationship. Abandonment at this stage would devastate the survivor.

Survivors, too, may wonder if they will ever retrieve the person they once knew as themselves. Their confusion frequently manifests itself in their sexual experience. In bewilderment, these survivors asked themselves:

> "Why am I turned on sexually and then I freeze?"

> "Why does anything that could lead to sex make me angry and make me want to crawl back in my shell?"

The confusion may manifest in other ways as well, such as around the issue of safety. The survivor will often possess intense feelings of insecurity, or of being "unsafe" during this period of discovery. These may escalate to the level of sheer terror, which is intense enough to be paralyzing. The survivor may be afraid to go out of the house, drive a car, or carry out normal social interactions. Such behavioral changes can alter family interactions, as well as the management of daily life (schedules, tasks, etc.).

Feelings of insecurity can also provoke hypervigilance, an intense watchfulness. (More will be said about this in Chapter 5) This behavior can take on the appearance of paranoia and may thus affect all the interpersonal relationships of the survivor, and most certainly impact the Partner. When such feelings arise anything the Partner can do to make things more secure for the survivor will be beneficial for both parties. He can reassure her of his love, his support, and his constancy, as well as respect her boundaries, and help her to honor and care for her body and its needs.

THE PARTNER'S FEELINGS

During the period of discovery the Partner will recognize opportunities to confront, and deal, with his own feelings about the abuse. He will likely feel everything from anger and rage to deep sadness. Although his partner is the one who is primarily wounded, he too may experience a sense of injury. He too, can never go back to his previous state of consciousness. His life is changed forever.

At this stage the Partner finds it hard to accept that once the initial discovery occurs, once the abuse is acknowledged, like Pandora's box in the myth, the lid on the memories of sexual abuse held in the unconscious can never be totally closed again. When the survivor has consciously or unconsciously decided to acknowledge that childhood abuse occurred, the decision can never be retracted, unless the survivor goes into total denial.

He or she can no longer ignore the feelings that have lain dormant in the psyche for many years. The channel has been opened for those feelings to emerge, and they may now come pouring out with little or no apparent conscious control, inundating both parties. Such feelings may include terror, rage, confusion, feeling little, loneliness, and numerous others. While many intense feelings will be evoked around sexuality and sexual activity, almost all aspects of the survivor's life will be affected. And, of course, the relationship itself will not escape the impact.

As a Partner, it was difficult for me to grasp at first why the mere mental awareness and understanding of the abuse did not automatically make everything all right. Why couldn't it just enable her to put everything back in its place and we could get on with our lives? Why couldn't she just let this make sense of her turmoil and upsets and then eliminate them?

Now, eight years later, as I write from the perspective of having lived through healing our lives, as well as dealing with my own new-found history as a survivor of abuse, I understand that it is not that simple. The survivor can **know** what is causing the problem but cannot voluntarily diminish the effects. One cannot pull away from the emotional interactions with the self or with the world by act of will. Those emotional reactions, the re-experiencing of emotions that arose and were repressed in childhood, really do seem to take on a life of their own. It is almost like having another person living inside you, **and you don't have control of that person!**

At this point, it does no good for the Partner to say things like: "Why don't you just let it lie?" "Why do you have to drag all this up?" "After all, it happened ten (or 20, 30, 40, 50) years ago. It is in the past—let it stay there." "Why do you have to bring it all up now? Forget it. Just go on being who you are."

Even if the Partner feels compassion, love and support toward the survivor, he may still feel confused about how to express those feelings. Many partners have expressed their confusion such as these:

> "I'm confused about which way to go that would
> be the most helpful."

> "I am confused as to what actions to take."

> "It's hard to think of her as a survivor."

What should he do now? Is it more helpful to be sympathetic? Should he be angry with the perpetrator? It is too easy to just become angry with the survivor for not having taken care of it long ago, and angry at the rejection he may be experiencing from the survivor as a result of it.

Confusion, chaos, mistrust, anger, dismay, fear, anxiety, and rejection all become common feelings for both the survivor and the Partner during this period of discovery. Such intense emotional pain often leads them into denial. Many wish they had never discovered the sexual abuse, or brought it out of the closet. They would like to pretend that the abuse never happened or that they don't know about it.

4

THE STRUGGLE
WITH
DENIAL

*

*"This never happened to me.
I just made it all up."*

To the uninitiated, the whole subject of sexual abuse seems like just another unpleasant sociological phenomenon. To the sexual abuse survivor, it is a psychological nightmare. For the couple who is living through the discovery and healing of the abuse wounds, it is a violent emotional roller coaster they cannot escape. Sometimes they would rather just deny it all.

Denial often begins in childhood when the abuse originally occurs and remains as a protective mechanism, survival system, until some time later in life when the person is strong enough to handle remembering the abuse. Unless the survivor has continuous recall of the abuse since it happened (for example if it continued into adolescence), the memories of the abuse are usually deeply repressed in the unconscious until somewhere in the thirties, forties or fifties. The classical profile of the discovering survivor is that of a woman in her early thirties, in a relationship, married or unmarried. Though in my practice I have seen a wide age range of survivors, from early twenties to late fifties, both male and female.)

The awareness of the childhood sexual abuse initially may come as vague perceptions of something wrong, something bad having happened, incomplete flashbacks, or strange reactions to seemingly common everyday experiences (see Appendix 1 for the John Dean Symptom Check list). This is the time when it is easiest to deny that the abuse occurred. When a client is struggling with denial, I sometimes use hypnosis to help the her recall what actually happened. Even then, after remembering specific incidents of being abused, the idea of sexual abuse is so abhorrent to many people, that they still wish they could deny it. They feel that they must have made it up, or that they must be crazy even to think that this kind of thing could have happened. In the beginning stages of treatment, I see people cycle in and out of denial. As a psychotherapist, I have learned to expect that initially about once every six weeks a client will attempt to deny that it ever happened. She will question the work she is doing in therapy, question whether she made it all up, and even question her own sanity. She needs reassurance that she would not have made up this particular type of horror story, that it is real, and that she was not to blame. Hear the differing levels of denial and fear in these statements made by survivors:

> "My father wouldn't do that."

> "I didn't believe that the way he touched me could affect my life so dramatically."

> "It wasn't like rape."

> "This stuff doesn't run me, only other people."

> "My mother could not possibly have done this!"
> (a male survivor)

THE EFFECTS OF DENIAL

Running

A survivor's denial can take different directions. If the survivor is in a relationship, she may simply run or find some excuse to end the relationship (for it is being in the relationship that has enabled the feelings to come up). She may create a series of very short-term relationships. That way she never has to deal with the feelings of fear that arise being in a truly intimate relationship. To the Partner, who loves her, the excuse to end the relationship will seem artificial, but he may blame himself for some unidentified error or terrible mistake and quiz her to identify that error. Or he may punish himself for all the little things he did or did not do that he can identify. However, they are not really the problem at all.

"Go Away!"

Another pattern that denial can take, is approach-avoidance behavior. The survivor seems to invite and want closeness and intimacy, yet when it occurs, she suddenly withdraws. She may engage in sexually intimate behavior with many different partners, trying to create the illusion of intimacy, but share no real intimacy with any of them. Such sexual behavior may be genital or may even remain non-genital. As a way of creating distance, she may accuse her Partner of being more interested in someone else and then use it as an excuse to end the relationship.

Eating Disorders

During the denial stage, if the survivor is bulimic (an eating disorder characterized by binging on food followed by purging, usually through self-induced vomiting or by use of laxatives) she will have more episodes of bulimia. It is a way of literally stuffing the feelings. Being full is a way of preventing the fear, anger, and other feelings from coming up. Dealing with feelings of embarrassment or guilt about being bulimic can conveniently mask the sexual abuse. It is worth noting that according to recent research, 90% of all bulimics were sexually abused as children.[1]

This pattern may be true of anoretics as well. If the survivor is anorexic she probably will go into a more acute phase. I remember my first encounter with anorexia many years ago while doing an internship at a large clinical hospital. One of the patients assigned to me was an 18 year old girl who had just delivered a baby. When I met, her she was not eating and was severely underweight. After several counseling sessions, her story slowly began to emerge. Everyone assumed her boyfriend was the father of the child, but in fact he was not. She had never slept with him. It was her stepfather who had impregnated her. Her denial of the sexual abuse was driving her into anorexia. She was slowly committing suicide. In those days the correlation between bulimia or anorexia and sexual abuse was less known, or at least was less public.

Somatic Disorders

Denial may take other somatic directions. Body symptoms emerge in the form of minor or even major illnesses. If the abuse is denied, then it is not okay to be in pain emotionally. The emotional pain becomes somatic. It gets converted to a more psychologically acceptable form, manifesting itself in the body in some way and some place that is more legitimate, such as muscular spasms, vaginal yeast infections, low back pain, or constipation. Such somatic expressions are common if the abuse was genital. If the abuse was more oral in nature (fellatio or cunnilingus), mouth infections may emerge. It can even appear as the common cold, or frequent respiratory disorders.

Psychological Disorders

Denial can result in more severe psychiatric symptoms. Depression is not uncommon, nor is Bipolar disorder (a manic-depressive reaction). Survivors may be suicidal or make suicidal threats during this phase. If so they may need professional care and support. Denial and repression may have been the mode of coping for so many years that when this defense begins to fall apart it can be very distressing. Borderline disorders occasionally appear. The sexual abuse so violates the child's personal boundary system, that it may permanently destroy it. Survivors sometimes lose the ability to distinguish between themselves and others. They occasionally even take on another's identity. In a relationship, they frequently don't know where their personal boundaries end and another's begin. This adds to the threat of being in a relationship and can further exacerbate the need to run. If this is dealt with in therapy and transference can be worked through, the survivor has a good chance of getting through it and coming out whole.

Workaholics

People in denial are often very hard-working. Coming from a place of low self-esteem, they may work harder than almost anyone else, in their attempt to prove their worthiness or their value as human beings. As one woman expressed it:

> "I can admit I was abused only if I work hard (VERY HARD), to save other people. I can accept my success only if I overwork. I can only be happy if I agree to mess it up later, (e.g. by becoming exhausted, then angry!)."

We live in a culture that usually rewards hard work. If their hard work is sufficiently rewarded they may become what is known as "workaholics." They are always working, never allowing themselves adequate time for rest, let alone time for play. Work can be as addictive a "drug" as alcohol and can mask the abuse, thus furthering the denial. By staying busy they don't have time for their feelings. Men may be more susceptible to such addiction than women, as the world tends to reward them for their working behaviors more than women.

Workaholics sometimes put on a very brave front for the world, genuine to almost everyone, including themselves. They adopt an attitude of being able to handle anything, that says: "I don't have any limits." They genuinely may not know their limits, nor where their boundaries reside.

This same type of denial may occur in the Partner. Psychologically he may be a very mature individual, and yet deny that the abuse will create any problems he cannot handle. To the Partner this whole period of time can be very distressing. The previously sane, loving, "normal" human being whom he loved, now seems to be someone very different. It takes great courage for both survivor and Partner to live through this denial stage.

Denial in the Bedroom

During the denial stage, lovemaking may bring up the memories and the feelings associated with the sexual abuse. If that occurs, the survivor likely will have less interest in making love, and will try to keep it to the very minimum. I will say more about this later in Chapter 8. She may even find sex repulsive and entirely reject any approaches by her Partner. For the Partner the frustration of not being able to initiate sex successfully, produces anger and resentment. In his pain from rejection he may want to counter-reject. Yet that too produces fear. As one Partner put it:

> "I get so mad that I want to give her some of her own medicine. Yet I'm so afraid that if I say no to her when she is interested, it will be so long before we ever make love again, that I don't do it. And then I am mad at myself for being that way too!"

At this stage the Partner may direct his anger toward the survivor. Later, he may turn it toward the perpetrator. It is here that we encounter one of the stranger aspects of the abuse healing process: the survivor may feel the need to protect the perpetrator from the Partner and his anger. When he would like to attack the perpetrator, the survivor tries to protect him, especially if she has not yet confronted the perpetrator about the abuse. Partners in our workshops have found this shocking and bizarre.

I'm OK Now—a Form of Denial!

Another form of denial that masquerades as recovery is frequently reflected in statements such as: "Yes, I was abused, but I am OK now." Therapist-survivors may be especially susceptible if they have not completed their own healing work. Hear the denial and confusion in this therapists words:

> "I'm done working on this. I've worked through
> my assault. I'm in control, so why the fuck is all
> this stuff re-emerging now?"

The problem lies, not so much a denial of the sexual violation itself, as in the denial of the effects of the violation. Healing sexual from abuse is hard work. It easily becomes quite time consuming (possibly obsessive) and interferes with life's other activities. While it is important to get on with life, we cant ignore the vital roll of the healing work. As we will see later in the section on bargaining, survivors sometimes say, "yes it happened to me, but I don't need to deal with it," or "I've already dealt with it." This very deceptive form of denial forces the abuse and its effects farther underground.

Couple Collusion

A more subtle form of denial is what I call couple collusion. Here the couple has acknowledged the abuse to themselves, but that is as far as they have gone. They may never have told anyone else, not even their own children. Of course if their children are young, less than ten years old for example, it is probably not appropriate to tell them. But if their children are adolescents or adults, keeping it a secret from them may not be healthy, and may only be a further form of denial.

BREAKING THE DENIAL PATTERN

One effective way to break the denial pattern is simply to tell another human being about it. Start with someone you trust, such as a therapist or a close friend. Telling other family members may not be so easy, when you first step out of denial. Once you have told others they become allies in helping both survivor and Partner avoid the denial. Once you tell others about the abuse and the effects it has been having on you and your relationship, you will find it harder to slip back into denial again. You may not be ready to confront the perpetrator yet, but you have taken a significant step along the healing path. You cannot heal a problem when you do not acknowledge its existence.

BARGAINING

Many survivors would prefer to forget that the sexual abuse ever happened. In fact, many people in their lives, including family members, will suggest they do just that. They will say, "It happened so long ago, why don't you just forget it, and let bygones be bygones? Why do you have to drag out all that old stuff again?" Most of the time, survivors would like nothing better than to be able to do that. But it doesn't work, so they have to find some other way of handling it. Once you acknowledge that you can't make your awareness of the sexual abuse go away, how do you cope with it? Some survivors attempt to make inner bargains with themselves as a way of coping with the pain such as: "I'll agree that it happened, if I don't have to deal with it . . . ever!" Or they may attempt to make bargains with their Partner, especially around the issue of sex.

"Why can't we just adopt a child and forget sex
for a while?"

Bargains like these are not "bargains" at all, and usually end
up being destructive to the survivor and to the couple. Sometimes
Partners would also like to make some bargain with themselves or
the survivor or both—anything to lessen the pain! One Partner
told his wife:

"I can be patient if you will try harder to deal
with sex."

PARTNER IMPATIENCE

Sometimes those inner or outer bargains don't seem to be
enough. Some Partners feel very impatient and angry with the
pace of healing. In their anger they may even blame the survivor
for what happened. One Partner told his wife:

"You asked for it! It was your fault that it happened. You could have stopped it. You were old
enough to stop it." (She was raped repeatedly at
age 14 while living in an orphanage.)

This kind of treatment only intensifies the guilt the survivor
may already feel about what happened. I think we constantly need
to remind ourselves, whether we are survivor or a Partner, that **no
child is responsible** for sexual activity that takes place with an
adult. The adult is the person responsible. It makes no difference
whether that child is four or fourteen years of age. It is well
known that children sometimes engage in sexual exploration **with
other children** to satisfy their curiosity about their bodies and
body functions. But curiosity cannot be used as an excuse by an
adult to justify sexual activity with a child. An adult who "ex-
plores" a child is violating the boundaries of that child and mo-
lesting that child. I am including here, in the definition as adult,

anyone who is in a trusted caretaker role. This includes teenage babysitters.

Many survivors torment themselves with feelings of guilt even if they receive no accusations from their Partners. They wonder if they might have done something to cause it, or if they did nothing to try to stop the abuse. Hear the anguish of the survivors in these statements:

> "Why didn't I tell someone? If I would have told sooner, surely it would have stopped."

> "Maybe I did do something (to cause it)."

> "I let him keep coming back, if only he'd stop hitting me. I wanted love so badly and thought that was it."

Yes, children need love. All people do. Adults can sometimes convince a child of the lie that an adult having sex with a child is love. While there may be elements of tenderness or kindness involved in the experience, it is still a long way from the kind of caring, supportive love that a child needs to grow and mature. Inappropriate sexual experience at a young age does not meet those needs. It only serves to confuse and distort the perceptions of the child. It psychologically wounds the child.

When a Partner blames the survivor for the abuse or for not stopping the abuse, he gets in the way of progress in healing. When the impatient Partner demands that the survivor just "forget it," he not only impedes the healing process, but makes it worse for himself as well. It only prolongs the pain. If the Partner's impatience is too strong the survivor may feel unsafe and forced to suppress the abuse again, to go back into denial, stopping the healing process completely. Partner impatience is one of the biggest reasons that survivors want to stop their healing. They are afraid that their Partner can't handle it. Being sensitive to their Partner's needs, they are afraid that if they continue their healing work, it will destroy the relationship.

HYPER-VIGILANCE

Survivors become hyper-vigilant for any type of threat to themselves. That deep, almost unconscious sense of being unsafe in childhood may carry on into their adult lives. They are constantly on the watch for anything that puts their safety in jeopardy, including the safety of their primary relationship. When they perceive their Partner as unable to cope with their abuse, they may want to stop the healing process, in order to protect their primary relationship. They may give in to their Partner's demands and pretend to themselves that it is not so important after all, using a thought like this to convince themselves: "If the abuse happened when I was three years old, I can forget it now." They think that maybe they really can just forget it. Wrong! This only pushes the abuse into the unconscious and allows it to impact the person and the relationship in ways that are unknown to both.

If the impatience of the Partner pressures the survivor to the extent that she begins to shut down her healing process, it will have a negative effect on the survivor and her primary relationship. Hard as it may be, one of the greatest gifts the Partner can give to the survivor is patience. When coupled with love, support and understanding, patience enables the survivor to heal at the fastest possible rate.

The Partner's question about when the turmoil will end is certainly a natural one, born out of his frustration and pain. But it is one that is best kept to himself. Probably the most honest thing any survivor can say to that question is: "I don't know!" Hopefully the Partner's love and support is not conditional, nor dependent on a time frame for the healing to end. Again let me assure the Partner that the pain will lessen. It is the nature of our humanity that healing brings release from pain. Healing the wounds of sexual abuse is no exception.

1. Phillips, Wayne, MD, *Psychological Trauma; A Major Cause of Mental Illness*, Centennial Peaks Hospital, Louisville, CO, 1989.

5

RUNNING
AWAY

*

*"I never feel safe! I'm running til I die,
running from this tormenting pain.
How do I get away?
Where do I go?"*

E scape behavior, such as running away from relationships, is
one of the most confusing, and least understood phenomena
in the whole sexual abuse picture. the importance and power
of this phenomenon, as well as its profound impact on the survivor and her relationships, should never be underestimated.

*As described in Chapter 2, whenever my fiancee and I began
to get emotionally intimate, she would periodically withdraw,
leave town, or end the relationship. Although she seemed out-
wardly to welcome closeness or intimacy, on another level it was
apparently a threat. What I now understand is that the closer we
became, especially if that closeness took on some characteristics
of "home," the more threatening the relationship became to her.
While this was most noticeable before our marriage, it also re-
mained true for several years after our marriage, until the abuse
became known to us and we could begin healing it. At that time
the escape behavior took the form of repeated threats to leave the*

relationship, which occurred at least monthly, and sometimes weekly for several years.

While getting into an emotionally intimate relationship is usually desired by the survivor, it is paradoxically often quite threatening, because it has taken on some of the characteristics of the "intimate" environment in which the abuse first occurred. Frequently, in such a relationship, the survivor feels unsafe without understanding why she is feeling that way. **When the survivor feels unsafe, there is an incredibly powerful urge to run.** To the survivor it can feel like a life or death matter. If she stays, she feels like she is going to die! While this may not seem rational, the feeling is there and is very, very powerful.

WHEN HOME IS NO LONGER SAFE

The urge to run away makes sense when we examine the background and source of these feelings. If the incest or abuse took place in the home, then any environment that begins to resemble "home" becomes a potentially dangerous place for the abuse survivor. This includes the physical surroundings as well as the people. When survivors set out to create their own living space, their own nest, unconsciously they often create something similar to the home in which they grew up. But soon they notice that it does not "feel right" (because of its similarity to the place of abuse). Still, since their childhood home is their primary model, they repeatedly create something like that model in their attempts to make a home. However, their good feeling about that new place, with its sense of rightness and safety, is frequently short-lived. Hence there is a constant quest for a better or nicer place to live and one with a different ambiance. Similarly, their quest for the right partner (read "safe!") is likely to be frustrated. This unconscious inner drive for safety can propel the survivor into a nomadic existence, either in terms of her place of residence or her relationships. As one survivor put it:

"Now I'm in a wonderful relationship, a wonderful place in my life. How am I going to ruin it? I don't deserve it. I'll destroy it. He really doesn't love me anyway. He's just pretending."

It is a such a crazy paradox! The more effort the survivor and Partner put into creating the home they want and a safe place for the survivor, the more it can be doomed to feel unsafe, **until they have healed the wounds of abuse.** Basically, home never feels safe to the survivor in the earlier stages of healing because home was not safe in childhood. In the beginning phases of healing, or in the pre-discovery stage, the survivor is unconsciously searching for a safe place. Whenever her place of living begins to take on a feeling of "home," then it begins to feel unsafe, a paradox seems like an impossible double-bind. The good news is that once your healing is well along, you can find or create a safe place. The nucleus of that safe place is, of course, essentially inside yourself. It can't be found anywhere else.

VARIATIONS ON THE THEME

Running away appears in other forms as well. It is common for survivors to have "long distance" relationships in which the love partner lives in another city or even another country. This provides the emotional distance necessary to sustain the relationship and prevents that sense of closeness or permanence that would begin to feel unsafe. While there may be periods or episodes (visits) in which there is extreme intimacy with intense and exciting sexual activity, the relationship is essentially safe from ever establishing that "home" environment that is so threatening. If the survivor makes the "mistake" of moving ahead with marriage to this long-distance lover before doing her healing work, she may be in for a lot of emotional and/or marital turmoil. The relationship may not seem "right." She will find many very rational reasons for her position. She may end the relationship and go on to repeat the pattern of having safe long-distance relationships until she heals.

Another variation depicts the survivor who never stays home. Home is just a place she checks into from time to time, or a place where she sleeps. In this pattern she may be away from home all day long, and most evenings too, at work and other activities. Or she may travel a lot in her work so her home functions more like another hotel room, with just a few personal touches. This life style, while safe, doesn't support living in an intimate relationship very well.

Unfortunately, it often seems that the adult survivor cannot **even get in touch with the abuse** (especially if it has been repressed since childhood) until she is in a strong, permanent relationship. For it is only in such a safe relationship that there is enough emotional stability for the abuse to begin to surface. For that very reason the survivor may do all kinds of things to circumvent forming such a permanent relationship and thus unconsciously keep the abuse unknown.

This sense of threat or insecurity can appear mysteriously in other ways too. Hypervigilance, common among survivors, operates like a computer search. The survivor is constantly watching and evaluating the environment and the people in it for any similarities to the features of the environment in which the abuse occurred. It could be a tent flapping in the wind, a pattern of light and shadows on a ceiling, the texture of a garment or bedcover, certain lighting conditions, certain sounds, tone of voice, how a person smells, etc. Those similarities may bring on terror or other unusual and unexpected emotional reactions. Moments of terror or uneasiness may appear at odd and inappropriate times and will be a complete mystery to the survivor and to her spouse, Partner, or friends. With healing, these unexpected reactions will diminish, though they may never totally disappear. But the survivor can recognize them for what they are and cognitively deal with them, without allowing them to rule her life.

Stand and Face the Dragon

But how do you get to the level of healing where the fear does not interfere with your life? How do you as survivors and Partners deal with this phenomenon, this urge to run, in healing your relationship? A principle in martial arts and in psychology is that the most useful strategy you can take is to "stand and face the dragon." This means you must confront your fears head on. If you find yourself engaged in a pattern of running whenever you become threatened, you must force yourself at some point not to run in order to break the pattern. The relationship you are in now may not be "the one" for you, but it can be useful in helping you to grow. If it has brought up the impulse to run, it will no doubt serve well the purpose of helping you confront your fears.

HEALING THE FEAR

I want to acknowledge that this is not a simple issue, nor an easy one to address. If you are reading this book together as a couple, the Partner can help the survivor to confront this fear. You must do all you possibly can to reassure her that it is safe here for her. Help her to focus on the feelings she is having and enable her to work through them.

Don't Underestimate the Dragon!

Understand that the need to run is a **very powerful feeling state.** Statements the survivor makes about the relationship that seem excessively critical can be taken as expressions of that feeling state rather than statements of fact about the relationship.

> "This relationship just feels all wrong!"

> "If I could just live in an apartment next door and you could stay in your house, I think I could get along just fine with you!"

Do not discount the feelings or the power of them. All of us need to feel safe. Feeling unsafe is a terrible way to have to live and cannot be tolerated for long. People will jump out of burning buildings so that they wont be burned alive by the fire, even though they know the jump will mean certain injury or even death. The need for safety in relationships is equally as powerful!

Getting "Space"

Acknowledge that any two people in a relationship may have different needs for closeness as well as for space. We all have differing needs for intimacy and closeness and differing needs for personal space. Generally, survivors of childhood sexual abuse will have a greater need for personal space than those not abused. The "distance factor" of a survivor may also be influenced by the life style she had before coming into the relationship, or from the model she saw with her parents. If the survivor has adequate "space" for herself, she may be capable of more intimacy.

Take the desire to run as a bid for space, and find some alternative ways to create space in the relationship. Some survivors have found that going for a drive in the country, in the mountains, or by the ocean is helpful. Making contact with nature is very grounding. If you live in a large city, perhaps going for a walk in a park, along a river or a beach, or another favorite place will help. Try finding an apartment or house with extra space, such as an extra room where you can hang out alone sometimes.

Having personal space was and is a great help for us in maintaining our relationship. When I could acknowledge that here was a woman who needs more space than I do, I found we could both be more comfortable. I discovered new possibilities for my own life as well. While it was necessary for me to redefine what space meant in a good relationship, I also found more personal freedom. We find it helpful to sometimes take a day apart to go off by ourselves. Occasionally one or the other of us will even sleep in the guest room for a night, without it meaning that our marriage is on the rocks.

Some survivor participants in our workshops have said: "I just think I am a person who needs more space than he does!" Survivors are often sensitive, creative persons, and thus they are more prone to get overloaded with interpersonal or environmental stimuli. When that happens, they need more space.

Sexual abuse violates the normal interpersonal boundaries of the growing, developing child and sets up confusion and uncertainty about interpersonal boundaries in adult life. Every human being needs to be able to establish and maintain boundaries. Without them we can become psychotic or crazy. When boundaries are uncertain or confused, having more personal space is one way to feel more secure around the issue of boundaries. When an intimate relationship develops, the survivor may feel her boundaries threatened and unconsciously sense that the only way to maintain her boundaries is to escape or run.

When the survivor and Partner understand the powerful feelings around the escape behaviors, the need for the survivor to act them out diminishes and the Partner can become more tolerant and supportive. The depth of fear that lies beneath the escape behaviors can then be faced. In facing it you can overcome it. You are not condemned to repeat it forever. You can create good relationships that can last! You can have a home in which you can be comfortable for more than a few weeks or months. You can be free of the need to run!

6

COPING
WITH
ANGER

✳

*"I am full of rage, pain & sadness and I
don't know why. That makes me angry too.
It's not just the incest, it's the fact that my
family worked overtime to make me out to
be crazy to keep the secret. How could
anyone be so cruel? I feel RAGE
when I realize this."*

A cknowledging sexual abuse in one's life opens the door to
feeling an incredible amount of anger, by or both the survivor and the Partner. This puts you both in a difficult position, for we live in a culture that does not readily support either
the feeling or the expression of anger. Yet if we do not express
anger appropriately and release or transform it, it will poison and
even destroy our most cherished relationship, as well as our happiness. Healthy couples healing from sexual abuse experience a
lot of anger throughout the healing process. You will both feel
angry with the abuser for what he or she did to you and the effect
it has had on your lives. You'll both feel angry with your/her par-

ent(s) for not protecting you, for not realizing what was happening to you and doing something about it.

As a survivor you'll feel angry with anyone who:
- left you alone with your abuser,
- should have been concerned and wasn't or who didn't act,
- didn't believe you when you tried to tell them what was happening when you were a child, such as teachers, ministers, relatives, parents, etc.,
- tells you to forget it, to let it stay in the past.
- blames you for the abuse,
- tells you that you did it for your pleasure, that you asked for it. [1]

As a Partner you may feel angry at:
- the gigantic disruption, turmoil, and pain you are feeling in your relationship,
- the loss you experience in your sex life,
- the loss of happiness,
- the anxiety and fear you find in your relationship.

In our culture we have few good role models for the healthy expression of anger. Dysfunctional families in which abuse occurs certainly don't provide that training. What we see on television or in the movies seems not much better. We can't throw down the gauntlet and challenge the perpetrator to a duel, though that might be a delicious fantasy. But we may engage in silent emotional duels that leave us almost as wounded as if we were using swords!

Some survivors have found an outlet for their anger by bringing the perpetrator to court and letting the court punish him/her. After all it is against the law to sexually abuse a child. Several such court cases have been recently reported. In one case reported on the CBS evening news in late April, 1990, the three adult children of one abusive couple filed charges, and both parents were sentenced to 15 years in jail. But both the mother and father were still denying the abuse as they were escorted away in handcuffs.

And in Denver on May 17, 1990, two daughters were each awarded $1.2 million in damages for being sexually abused by their father many years ago. They were now 44 and 45 years old, and he was 72 at the time of the judgment. The jury determined that even though the statute of limitations for a civil suit is two years, the sisters had only become aware of the nature and extent of their injury only during the past two years during therapy. Going through the courts often entails a long, arduous and expensive legal process, and charges are difficult to prove when the abuse took place years ago. Statutes of limitations vary from state to state. Often it is difficult for criminal charges to be filed. Proof becomes even more difficult if the abuser is regarded as an upright, responsible member of the community.

So what do you do with your anger? One survivor found some satisfaction by making her father pay for all her therapy after she had confronted him. How can you, as a couple, prevent the anger from spilling over onto each other, poisoning and polluting your relationship?

RECOGNIZE WHEN ANGER BECOMES DYSFUNCTIONAL

Dysfunctional anger patterns are more easily recognized in children than in adults. In a school classroom you might see a child who is angry hitting, acting out, kicking, fighting, stealing, hurting others or hurting animals. In addition you would probably observe a decline in classroom performance or lower grades. Adults who carry large loads of anger, often try to disguise it. With practice we can easily identify it in such behaviors as drinking, fighting, abusive shouting in the family environment, abusing animals, withdrawing and verbally attacking others. We might label such a person as anti-social. Work effectiveness will be reduced. In addition persons may abuse themselves, physically or emotionally.

DON'T USE ANGER AS PUNISHMENT

Anger is such a fascinating part of our human experience. Its primitive nature serves us in a fight-or-flight response to stress or threat. We can observe in ourselves some of the same kinds of responses we might see in our dog or cat (though slightly refined). Our instinctive response to perceived attack or injury is to strike back. Young children use their fists to express anger as they interact. Our four year old often hits when she is angry, even though we are doing our best to teach her not to hit.

Many adult survivors and their Partners feel a spontaneous desire to punish or strike back. Most people hold a belief that the world should be fair and sexual abuse certainly is seen as unfair! They resent the unfairness of it all. Survivors and Partners alike ask: "Why me?" The desire to punish or get even is present in most people and in our pain we plot revenge. I am not sure that we can ever train it out of ourselves completely. Even the most highly spiritual people may still feel it. Most of us have learned to monitor and temper our expression of the desire to punish, the need for revenge, and don't act it out in socially unacceptable ways. And how much punishment would be enough? If the perpetrator is sentenced to many years in jail or fined millions of dollars, the pain is still there and the psychological and emotional healing is still required.

As children growing up we came to associate anger with punishment. Our parents were frequently angry when they punished us, and now as parents, we are often angry when we punish our own children. So it is with good reason that anger is associated with punishment.

BARRIERS TO EXPRESSING ANGER

People in our culture generally have little internal or external permission to express anger. Thus suppressed anger can lead to abuse within the family and may come from either partner. Wives and children get physically abused because of it. Husbands, children, and wives get emotionally abused by each other. When we are dealing with the subject of sexual abuse, the situation is aggravated and we experience many barriers to expressing anger. Here are some of the most common barriers:

Fear of the Perpetrator

When sexual abuse occurs in childhood, the child usually feels powerless to do anything about it. The perpetrator helps create this condition by making threats to the child, such as: "Don't you tell! If you do I will (beat you, hurt your mom, kill you, etc.)!" One survivor recalled this insidious threat:

> "He said if I told Mom she would leave us. I was terrified she'd be so mad she'd leave me with him. That would be worse than putting up with the current level of abuse."

Children are not only afraid of telling anyone about their experience, they are afraid of expressing their rage. Families in which sexual abuse occurs, are usually dysfunctional anyway, **especially** in the area of expressing feelings and getting personal needs met. Such an environment does not encourage family members to be direct about individual feelings or needs. Fear of retaliation by the perpetrator is a very powerful inhibitor for the child, and may remain so for both the survivor and the Partner in their adult lives.

In my own case it kept me silent for 50 years. The woman who was my perpetrator threatened to kill me by suffocating me with a pillow. Then she proceeded to demonstrate how she would do it by holding a pillow over my face until I was almost suffocated before removing it. She made a believer of that little child I was at age four. The effects of that threat held the abuse silent, but not inactive, in my unconscious for half a century. As I have begun to talk about it, it has given rise to considerable fear.

When the child grows up the threat of retaliation by that parent or relative is still functioning in the unconscious. The old childhood proscriptions are still in place and operative. The child, now an adult, fears retaliation in the form of further rejection, harassment, disinheritance, disownment, and alienation from the rest of the family. One survivor experienced that alienation when she confronted her father in a letter. He retaliated by turning other family members against her, swearing that she was crazy and lying. He threatened to sue her for defamation of character. She feared he might even come beat her up. It became a very emotionally difficult and fearful time for her.

Fear that Anger Is Dangerous!

Pre-school age children move into quick and violent rages, which usually don't last more than a few minutes. At that age we have much less mental control over our emotions and our actions, and we easily break things or hurt people with our rageful hitting, kicking, and throwing. If the adults in our lives don't handle our anger very well, we may learn that our anger is dangerous and can hurt others. At a later age we convert this into fear of hurting others emotionally, especially in dysfunctional families in which individuals do not take responsibility for their own emotions and upsets. So we carry the belief that we can seriously hurt our parents or other family members all the way into adulthood. We use this fear to control our anger. Hear the fears of this woman:

> "If I tell, he'll only deny it or maybe he'll have a heart attack and die, and then I'd be responsible for his death, even if no one knows about the abuse. I couldn't live with that!"

Fear of Violence or Losing Control

As just mentioned, we fear that our anger will get out of control, become violent, and that we will hurt someone.[2] They think: "If I get angry, I get violent." Some individuals carry this to extremes, fearing that in their rage they might become homicidal and actually assault the perpetrator. It is not unusual for survivors to feel and even say in their rage, "I could just kill him!" Down underneath there is some fear that they might just do that, given the right opportunity, though most know they won't. Sometimes they may generalize their anger and violent thoughts to other people, such as this woman did:

"I'd like to cut off his (and all men's) balls"

A similar fear of losing control is frequently there for the Partner too, as he deals with his anger and rage at the perpetrator for having violated his loved one. Their thoughts sometimes contain statements of violence:

"I want to go kill the sonuvabitch!"

Fear of Repeating The Pattern

Survivors often vow to themselves that they will never abuse their own children. One woman survivor was so fearful, that when her boys were babies, she was sometimes afraid to change their diaper or bathe them, finding it hard to identify the line that separated caretaking from invading. There is some reality to these fears, in that all of us tend to replicate what we had modeled for us in childhood. We will tend to parent as we were parented. Abusers sometimes do come at the victim in anger, which frightens the survivor, striking terror in their hearts that can arise years later. Consequently, maintaining an awareness of what the abuser was like, can enable the survivor to refrain from repeating that same negative pattern.

DEALING WITH YOUR FEARS

Handling your anger is very important. While it is important to maintain awareness of your boundaries, and the limits you wish for your anger, it need not totally impede you from expressing your anger. True, you don't want to hurt anyone else, or to become like the abuser. Nor do you want to be naive about the possibility of retaliation, because it could be a real risk. Any of the items mentioned above, while useful to consider and keep in mind, can be carried too far. When that happens it becomes oppressive. You are then more likely to bottle up your anger and make it destructive to yourself.

FOUR PRECAUTIONS IN
DEALING WITH YOUR ANGER

I am grateful to Beverly Engel for an excellent chapter on anger in her book, *The Right to Innocence.*[3] In it she mentions three things not to do with anger: suppression, repression and displacement. I would like to flesh out those concepts and add a fourth.

Don't Suppress It By Ignoring It

In our culture the most common style of dealing with anger is to ignore it, hoping it will just go away. We hang on to this strategy because it sometimes works, for a while. If you find yourself angry on Monday, by Wednesday you probably won't be so angry. Other events will come along in your life and claim your attention, and you will "forget" it. But you know it is only a temporary fix. It is not an effective strategy for really managing your anger.

To suppress your anger means to forcefully put it down, to consciously dismiss it from your mind. It is a tool or strategy that can be temporarily helpful in special situations. If you let your anger spill forth anytime it arises, it can be counterproductive. When you are at work with your boss, a customer, or fellow workers is not the time to blast out with your anger, especially when the people you are really angry with are the ones associated with your abuse and are not present. The trouble is, if you do not address your anger with the abuser, you are more at risk of letting your anger out at inappropriate times. Use suppression of your anger sparingly, and only as a temporary measure.

Don't Repress It By Denying It

Repression means to force your anger down into the unconscious part of your mind until you are no longer even aware of its presence. It doesn't even exist, to you at least! This is an even more destructive way of trying to handle the anger evoked by sexual abuse. Repressed anger can cause havoc in your body, creating all kinds of nasty problems. A variety of illnesses, physical or emotional, can result from such a strategy. Depression has long been regarded as caused by repressed anger.

Repression, however, is usually not a conscious act. We tend to do it when it is not safe to experience fully our present reality, including our anger. Abuse survivors often have totally repressed the experience of the sexual abuse, as well as their anger about it, pushing it far down into the unconscious because they were unable to handle it at the time it occurred in their childhood. But the memories and the feelings lie there, stored in the unconscious, affecting the person throughout their lives in ways unknown to them until the abuse is brought to consciousness. This is discussed in greater depth in Chapter 3. Repression is an unconscious tool for survival. Repression may have occurred if you find yourself denying that you are even angry, and doing it long enough that you yourself believe it.

Don't Displace It Onto Others

Webster defines displacement as a defense mechanism in which an emotion is transferred to another, more acceptable object. A classic (though cliched) example of this is the man who gets mad at his boss and comes home to kick the dog. In your everyday life you are more likely to *displace* your anger onto your spouse, your children, or other family members. Both the survivor and the Partner are susceptible.

When recall of sexual abuse emerges later in life, it creates confusion. The perpetrator, who is most often a family member, (father, mother, brother, sister, uncle, etc.) is usually someone who also has been loved and revered. How can you now suddenly feel deep rage at that person for abusing you, and at the others for not protecting you? These feelings of intense anger seem incompatible with your other feelings of love and respect. This double bind is made worse when the perpetrator is dead, as is often true when the survivor discovers the abuse later in adult life. This survivor felt confused and angry because he was dead and she could not confront him:

> "How do you get angry at someone who is dead?
> I feel so confused."

> "I'm angry that he is dead and I can't confront him."

Displacing feelings of anger onto others (usually family members) is certainly an easy way to lessen internal conflict, though it may be destructive in the long run. And you may not be aware that you are doing it. Survivors and Partners in this situation sometimes have so much anger boiling inside them that they easily explode at minor irritations. Situations which normally would be handled calmly now become opportunities to blow off steam. One way to avoid doing this is to foster an awareness of when you are angry. Most of us do know when we are angry, though sometimes we are unwilling to acknowledge it even to ourselves. One of the easiest and most effective ways to handle this is to simply admit it to those around us. Try saying: "I am angry inside right now, and it has nothing to do with you, so don't take it personally. I'm angry with *(name)*. I'll try not to direct it at you, but I need to feel it."

This lets your family members know about your internal state so they can either stay out of your way, or respond to you in a non-defensive way. Perhaps they can even help you to express it or deal with it. Expressing it cleanly helps prevent your anger from poisoning your relationships.

Don't Project Your Anger Onto Others

Projection is the unconscious process of ascribing to other persons one's own ideas, impulses, or emotions. Projection is more likely to occur when the ideas or feelings are considered undesirable or cause anxiety. Anger around sexual abuse certainly falls in this category. If you do not feel comfortable with your own anger, then it is possible for you to imagine that others around you are angry. In effect you try to make them carry or act out the feelings you are having. Such projection could stimulate them to be genuinely angry . . .at you!

CREATIVE APPROACHES TO ANGER

Many books are now available on anger (see the bibliography). I do not want to try to duplicate here the fine work already done or create an anger "cookbook." I do want to share with you some of my thinking about anger and share a few of the things that have worked well for my wife and me. Many of the current anger releasing techniques are cathartic in nature, that is, they encourage you to "get the anger out." Techniques such as shouting, using foam bataca bats or tennis racquet to hit pillows do get it out. While I believe there is a place for this kind of work, some recent research shows that such techniques may in fact perpetuate the anger, rather than release it.

Your Anger Is OK

You can learn that your anger is not dangerous, that it is safe and healthy to experience. Giving yourself some controls and outlets for your anger is a way of helping yourselves through your angry stages. As a couple you can help each other by observing when your partner is angry. First, when you sense anger present, ask him or her if he/she is aware of feeling angry. Sometimes our anger is there without our being consciously aware of it. Often by merely calling our attention to it, we can allow ourselves some release. A second step is to invite your partner to tell you what he or she is angry about. It may be something quite existential . . . present day, or it may be from the past about the abuse. By doing this you acknowledge the anger, and make it okay to experience it. It is way of communicating that it is okay to be angry. This too can be a release. A third step might be to engage in some form of problem solving if it is a current issue, or to ask what needs to be done about it.

Anger As Energy

One way of looking at anger is to see it as energy. When you get angry, your body responds by flooding your system with hormones, including nor-epinephrin and adrenalin. It gives your whole body a tremendous "kick," as it prepares you for the fight-flight response. With all those "juices" in your system you can work or play harder, and in fact you ought to in order to burn up those hormones so that you won't be left feeling nervous or sleepless. At that point, engaging in some physical activity such as tennis, racquetball, handball, biking, swimming or some other active sports could be very useful. A racquet sport also gives you a way to hit something and satisfy that primitive urge. Other forms of externalizing the anger include working in your garden, hiking, running, or going for a walk. But I believe that we must go farther than just releasing or using the energy.

Sublimation

The four non-productive strategies mentioned (suppression, repression, displacement, and projection) need to be replaced with something productive. These are all types of defense mechanisms. Sublimation may also be a defense mechanism, but it is the highest of them. Sublimation is a useful way to approach anger and means to express what IS unacceptable in a constructive, socially acceptable form or to purify or ennoble it. Sublimation is thus a transformational process. The ancient alchemists tried to take common elements and turn them into gold. As metaphor, we can be alchemists and transform the dross of anger into something valuable and useful. I believe it is possible to use anger for personal transformation.

Anger has been present on the human scene for many thousands of years. Some of the world's great teachers of the past, including Jesus, Buddha and Confucius offered mankind ways of handling anger that were transformative in nature. Surely modern western psychology hasn't found THE answer for anger management by suddenly discovering pillow pounding.

How to release anger is a choice that each person can make. After acknowledging your anger, admitting it to yourself and to others, you must then decide what you want to do with it. Does your anger serve you? It can. For instance, anger can serve both the survivor and the Partner by helping them create distance between themselves and the perpetrator. Because of the seductive nature of power in relationships with the perpetrator, the survivor often has difficulty saying no to that perpetrator, even in adult life when the demands are more likely to be emotional than physical or sexual. Anger can help you to say "no!"

If your anger is carried over to other people in your life, it may not be serving you, and may in fact get in your way. Between survivor and Partner, the anger may only function to distance you from each other when you least need it. In this case it goes against serving your needs for intimacy, companionship, and sexual expression. Ask yourself, is this wall my anger creates between us serving me? Clients tell me from time to time of instances when one will not speak to the other for hours, days, or weeks at a time as a means of punishment.

Each of us carries a composite myth in our head of what our partner should be for us. It is made up of all the ideal persons we've been exposed to in person, or in the movies. When we measure the real person against the composite myth, there is no way he or she can measure up to those expectations, nor can you yourself. We thus often expect our partners to behave in certain ways, and when they don't we get angry. Are you trying to punish your partner for not meeting your needs?

Having the humility to acknowledge our own imperfections enables us to allow our partner to have his shortcomings, and to appreciate what he does have to give us. Moving in this direction helps to transform the anger energy and keep it from poisoning our relationships.

Coming back to the sexual abuse, there is little doubt that you are justified in being angry, whether you are the survivor or the Partner of a survivor. At some point, however, you need to choose how long you want to hang on to your anger. Does it continue to serve you? Is it now useful, or is it getting in the way of your important relationships? You can choose to maintain your distance from the perpetrator without having to maintain an anger state to do it. Consider instead choosing to sublimate or redirect the energy from your anger (transform it) in positive ways. One woman started collecting art and poems by survivors to create a book for publication.

As an art therapist, my wife uses clay or resistive media such as oil pastels (a type of chalk) on cardboard to release anger. Here is how she sees it:

> "I think art is a form of sublimation. I can go in
> my studio and take crayons and pulverize paper.
> Or I can take that same energy and work on a
> painting I have in process and somehow let the
> energy move in my painting even when it is not a
> painting about anger. The anger merely becomes
> raw energy which I can use." [4]

Art also provides a safe vehicle for expressing fantasies of revenge (i.e., what you would like to do to the perpetrator or to those who did not protect you). There is a destructive, though healing, quality to art, literally tearing up the old (drawing, painting) to make way for the new. Clay is a wonderful medium for this expression. You can obtain a 25 lb. block of clay ($5-7) from your art supply store. You can pound it, tear it, squeeze it, or make images of the perpetrator and his family, and then attack the images. You can use the clay to create expressions of your own pain as well as anger.

I often envied my wife's ability to use her art materials to get at and express her feelings. Since I am not an artist, I used to think I could not do the same thing. Not long ago however, when I was in the midst of some particularly heavy feelings, I found that using some child's crayons and chalks and some paper, (materials accessible to anyone) I could make simple drawings that helped me to express my feelings. It was wonderful! You might try creating something together with your partner.

Converting Anger to Laughter

When we first began using this entertaining technique, we saw it primarily as a way to "get our anger out." Looking at it now, I realize it was also a way of transforming our anger . . . *into laughter!* This is a fun way to release anger. When we are feeling the need to engage with one another and to release anger, we play at "Growling!" We clear a space in the living room and get down on our hands and knees and begin to growl and snarl at one another as if we were animals. We make it sound as ferocious as possible, baring our teeth, and sometimes pushing at one another with our shoulders, though not hard enough to hurt each other. This may sound ludicrous to you, but it is wonderfully freeing. At the time we were using this the most, my teenage children were living with us. When they saw us doing this they were absolutely convinced their father and stepmother had "gone around the bend," and would give us "that look." Our dog, on the other hand, loved it! She would get so excited that she would start barking and growling too and sometimes try to intervene. At that point we would usually both end up rolling on the floor with laughter. You can't do this and remain totally serious. It is a wonderful release, however! Try it!

Journaling And Letter Writing

Keep a personal journal during your healing. Use it to express your thoughts, feelings, and ideas. Writing down your angry feelings is very useful. Write letters to the perpetrator which you don't plan to mail. It is a safe way to express the feelings of anger you have toward him. Mail them only if you are ready to confront him or have already done so.

DON'T ABUSE YOURSELF

Dealing with the wounds of sexual abuse will bring up anger, for both the survivor and the Partner. You can count on it! But don't abuse yourself or your relationship with your anger. Misdirecting your anger at yourself or your partner hurts both of you and your relationship. Self abuse may take many forms, from simply overworking to secret eating binges. Don't blame yourself for what happened. Remember, the abuse was not your fault. If you are a survivor, don't torment yourself with: "I could have stopped it if . . ." Recognize that as a small child you were powerless to do anything about it. Don't punish yourself now. Partners need to be very careful not to abuse or punish the survivor for it either. Use your anger energy as stimulus for productive activity. Transform the anger, channel it into directions that will enhance your life.

1. Engel, Beverly, *The Right to Innocence, Healing the Trauma of Childhood Sexual Abuse*. Tarcher, 1989, pg. 88,
2. *Ibid.*, pg 89.
3. *Ibid.*, pg. 89.
4. Mimi L. Farrelly, ATR, MA

7

GRIEF

✳

*"I felt like a volcanic explosion
during the day and would cry
my eyes out all night."*

Anger and grief remain companions throughout the healing process. They sometimes appear simultaneously, or at least close to each other in time. While it seems normal and natural for both the survivor and the Partner to feel anger at the perpetrator, it may seem strange when one or both of them begin feeling grief.

Neither party may identify the experience as grief at first. The individual will more than likely feel depressed, tired, listless, and despondent. Or feelings may not even be defined as specificly as that; he or she will be aware only of feeling badly. Life may not seem as worthwhile as it did before all this came up. Such feelings are normal, and reflect an appreciation of a certain sense of loss, or a state of grief.

WE GRIEVE FOR LOSSES

We normally associate grief with the type of loss we experience when someone close to us dies. It seems normal to cry and feel sad then. However, grief and tears are quite normal thorughout the healing process. There are real losses for both the survivor and the Partner, and perhaps for the relationship as well. Maybe it would be helpful to identify some of the losses. As a survivor of sexual abuse:

You Lost Your Happy Childhood

You lost, perhaps years of normal play and joy that should have been yours as a child. And you greive because, as one woman said sadly: "He took that little girl from me. He had <u>no</u> right to do that. How come no one saved me from him?" Sexually abused children commonly become mistrusting, sad, unhappy and withdrawn. For some it is almost like a death of the little child they were at the time the abuse occurred, as we hear in this poignant expression:

"Dear Dad, you killed your little girl!"

But what does that loss mean now? You are no longer a child. You are an adult. Does that still count? Yes, it does. For, when you've lost a happy childhood, you've lost the opportunity to progress normally through some very important developmental stages. Many adult survivors are compulsive hard workers. They have no concept of play, which they would have developed in a normal happy childhood. They can be heavy, dull, and boring to be around. Lightheartedness, an essential component of a well rounded adult, is just not there. This certainly has implications for the survivor's relationships, and will have an impact on his or her Partner.

You Lost Your Innocence

A sexually abused child is thrust into sexual experiences far in advance of being psychologically or physically ready for those experiences. In a manner of speaking, these children are *taught* to be sexual and to respond sexually. As teens or adults they may unconsciously act seductively with others and find it leads them into sexual activity that they neither deserve or want. They tend to sexualize normally non-sexual situations. They do not have the wisdom or maturity to discriminate appropriate from inappropriate behavior.

Families in our culture make considerable effort to keep a child "innocent" (uninformed or inexperienced) about sex and sexual activity. (Some of this is appropriate and helpful and some of it can later be inhibiting or counterproductive.) This innocence contributes some of the magic of the teenage years when the adolescent is exploring his or her own sexuality and that of the opposite sex as well. For the survivor of sexual abuse, if remembered, there is little magic. I remember well the moving statement of one young survivor reflecting her lost innocence:

> "When I was in high school and some girls were giggling and saying they could not imagine what it would feel like to have a boy's penis in their vagina, I couldn't join in the fun, and I couldn't wonder with them because I knew what it felt like already. I knew what my father's penis felt like in me when I was a young girl. It didn't feel good then. It just hurt!"

Other survivors have said:

> "I feel ripped off!"

> "I knew what it felt like to have my penis fondled and sucked on."

The Partner experiences loss here as well. When two persons have experienced sexual intimacy for the first time together, what had been regarded as a "virginal" experience, is now no longer that first experience. The abuse robbed them of that possibility, and is the source of a great loss. Their reality has been altered.

You Lost Your Ability To Trust Openly

When an adult says "I love you" and then proceeds to abuse a child, physically or sexually it creates pain and confusion. The child has previously associated being loved with being cared for, nurtured, and protected. Now being "loved" seems associated with pain, with feeling violated, blamed, invaded, terrorized and then threatened with punishment or even death. How confusing and traumatic this is to the child! It is life altering! Later, in adult life (whether the abuse is remembered or not), when a love partner says "I love you," the survivor may find herself or himself suddenly shrinking in terror, withdrawing from the relationship, or feeling anxious and threatened for no apparent reason. Such a time is confusing to both the survivor and the Partner. If they do not understand the source of this reaction, it can inhibit or possibly destroy the relationship. They may learn simply to dance around the issue, not saying the words, but eventually it will catch up with them.

A good relationship or marriage must begin with and build on a deep trust. Only in an atmosphere of openness and trust can we truly come to know who we are and allow ourselves to blossom and develop to our fullest potential. An intimate relationship provides the context for this trust, unless it is damaged by the trust having been violated at a young age.

You Lost Your Sense of Self Worth

Almost all children, even the most severely abused, develop some sense of what is right and wrong. This applies to sexual behavior as well as social behavior. Children know when something feels wrong. When they are told to keep sexual abuse a secret and are threatened if they don't, they know that the abuse is wrong. Many children feel guilty about the sexual abuse, and often feel they somehow caused it. Since in their world adults are supposed to know what is right and know all things, children feel *they* must be wrong or bad for this to have happened. Sometimes this belief

was a part of their known reality. Its absence sometimes creates discomfort and anxiety. Recent research shows that there are biochemical changes that take place in the human brain in response to trauma, especially if it occurs early in life. These changes create a certain discomfort and anxiety, that is relieved only by more retraumatization. Thus children will retraumatize themselves by head banging. Adults will sometimes mutilate themselves by cutting themselves or by getting into abusive relationships. In a strange way, such retraumatization creates a temporary relief.[1]

There are many, many other things lost as well, such as :
- respect and esteem from the Partner,
- feeling in control of one's feelings,
- normal mothering or fathering traits,
- self confidence,
- knowing what is a normal interpersonal reaction in relationships. Your sex life also may be adversely affected. (See Chapter 8.)

THE PARTNER GRIEVES TOO

It is not as easy to see the areas of loss for the Partner and understand his grief, but he too has losses.

He Loses "The Girl (Boy) That I Married!"

After the sexual abuse has surfaced the partner may ask: "What happened to the woman (man) that I married?" He feels like he has lost her. In her place is someone very different. Her personal history and background are now different. Her attitudes toward life, toward him, toward herself, her body, and toward sex are different. Hopefully there is still enough of her core self present, that he will not feel the need to go away or give up on the relationship. But there is real grief for the Partner around the loss of the person he married.

He Loses Years of Happiness

The Partner may lose significant or extended periods of happiness while as a couple they plow through the stages of healing. Here again it is important for the Partner to have his own support systems. He needs people with whom he can talk about his experience. He needs people with whom he can cry if need be, a support system of friends.

HEALING YOUR GRIEF

Healing grief is no easy process for either the survivor or the Partner. It may be lengthy or it may be brief, but it is an essential part of healing from sexual abuse. With all these losses by both parties, each needs to be sensitive and supportive of the other as they move into and through the healing process. Allow yourselves time to grieve. Be patient with each other around this part of your healing. Here are some essential elements of your grief process.

Cry! Cry! Cry!

Give yourself time: time to cry, time to brood, time to be quiet. You may find yourself crying at seemingly inconsequential stimuli. Just seeing a child playing in a normal fashion, or seeing old objects or pictures from your childhood may remind you of what you lost and bring tears. Realizing the extent of what you have lost will bring tears. Give yourselves permission to cry as much as you need to. You will eventually stop, though neither you nor your Partner may think so.

Indeed this is a critical stage of healing for the Partner and for the relationship. The Partner may feel frustrated and impatient with the survivor's crying. As one said: "All she does is cry all the time. Every time I come home she is back in the bedroom crying." Being impatient with the tears only aggravates the situation and slows down the healing. One of the best things the Partner can do is to continue to offer to hold the survivor as she cries. Support her so she can cry, cry, cry.

Talk About It!

Talking is an essential component of grief work. So talk about it! It is easy to say, and yet hard to do . . . both for the survivor and the Partner. Survivors are often embarrassed about their abuse. Their Partners also may be embarrassed or ashamed of the abuse. This can get in the way of using one of the most crucial tools for healing grief. Talk to your friends, to other survivors, to Partners, to anyone who will listen attentively and sensitively. Talk, Talk, Talk! Survivors need to encourage their Partners to talk about their losses too. Joining a support group may be helpful. If you can't find one, perhaps you can start one. You may even want to advertise in your local paper.

One of my friends, Dr. Bruce Fisher, who works with divorce adjustment, says, in speaking of the grief work of divorce: "You tell your garbage story until you run your friends off, and then you get another set of friends until you run them off too with your sad stories. Finally with your third set of friends, you have talked about it enough so you can keep them."[2] When we are dealing with emotionally traumatic experiences or significant emotional losses, talking about them is essential to healing. You must talk about your loss until you can stand to live with it, and then you won't need to talk about it so much. I think that's true of healing sexual abuse too. Survivors and their Partners must talk about it until they can stand to live with it. Then they won't need to talk about it . . . at least not as much.

Rituals That Heal

In our culture we have developed certain rituals and ceremonies for dealing with grief. When someone dies we hold a funeral or memorial service. Sometimes a wake is held where friends can come by to see the family and express their condolences. When people retire they are often given some sort of celebration to honor the years of service. In some cultures people wear black clothing, and hold elaborate social and religious ceremonies at times of death. Creating some type of ritual or ceremony that honors and gives additional permission for grieving that which is lost can be very helpful. If that loss is your innocence, your childhood, it is worthwhile to hold that ritual. Let me tell you how one person did that.

Near the close of her therapy, I assisted a client as she developed her own ritual to heal her losses. She made a small but elaborate wood box about 10" x 12" x 4". In this box she placed some small figures she had made out of pipe cleaners and other materials that represented herself and her father. They were place in sexually explicit positions in the box. With them she placed some photos of her father and a mask she had made that portrayed her cry of anguish. The mask represented her victimhood. Next we conducted a Native American medicine wheel ceremony that included a time for releasing of negative energies and for renewing herself. Then the box was set afire and burned to ashes which were swept away by the wind. Somehow grief needs acknowledgment to become complete. It needs to be publicly witnessed, even if only by one other person. That is what funerals, religious or social rituals provide for the important rites of passage in our lives, such as deaths, weddings, baptisms, etc. With this public acknowledgement the survivor or Partner can more readily let go of that which is lost and complete the grief work. You may want to consider creating and sharing a ritual with your partner and/or others to help you bring closure to your grief.

Write About It

I spoke of journaling in the previous chapter on anger. Writing about the grief you are experiencing inside you also can be very healing. I recommend that you keep a journal throughout your healing process. Share excerpts with your partner only when you feel ready. It is primarily for you. I have suggested some aspects you may have lost, personally and as a couple, due to your abuse, but you need to make that specific for yourself. Take time right now to identify clearly in your mind and write down what you have lost, whether you are a survivor or a Partner. When you feel you have covered the subject thoroughly enough, then share what you have written with your partner or friends or family. In conclusion, it is important to acknowledge that you have had losses and that you deserve to grieve those losses. Only through that grieving can you heal the pain of your loss and reach that place of wholeness and peace you seek. Out of your grieving can emerge a new and stronger relationship.

1. Bessel A. van der Kolk, The Trauma Spectrum: The Interaction of Biological and Social Events in the Genesis of the Trauma Response, *Journal of Traumatic Stress*, Vol. 1, No. 3, 1988, pg 273 ff.

— Bessel A. van der Kolk, MD, *The Compulsion to Repeat the Trauma: Re-enactment, Revictimization, and Masochism,* Psychiatric Clinics of North America – Vol 12, No. 2, June 1989, pg. 389 ff.

2. Fisher, Bruce, *When Your Relationship Ends.*

8

SEX

*

S ex! That part of our human experience that is the subject of more movies, more jokes, and more interest than any other, becomes the source of pain for many survivors and their partners. For survivors a real dilemma is created because of the conflicting feelings that arise. Their normal adult feelings of arousal, excitment, and orgasm, occur simultaneously with the feelings of the child that was abused, such as fear, shame, guilt, powerlessness, and being out of control. The following statements from two women survivors captures this painful and poignant dilemma exquisitely:

> "When I become aroused, I'm scared about how
> I'll react or I feel ashamed to be aroused at all."

> "If he's on top I feel suffocated. If I'm on top, I
> feel like I caused it all and I feel like a whore. I
> can't win."

A couple's sexual relationship is often the first noticeable part of the relationship affected by the wounds of child sex abuse. When the survivor has not remembered or acknowledged the abuse, the disturbance of a couple's sex life may be especially severe. Sex is such a difficult topic to talk about when the relationship is in trouble. Both for men and for women, much of what happens in their sexual relationship deeply affects their self esteem. There are few like to admit that their sex life is frustrating, painful, or is nonexistent. Probably the most common experience of survivors and Partners, whether they know about the abuse or not, is to notice their sex life diminish and almost disappear. Couples who enjoyed making love daily or several times a week in the first few months of their relationship, find that they don't make love for days or weeks at a time. That classic cartoon of the wife complaining "honey, I have a headache" does actually happen. What was an enjoyable and vital part of their relationship at the beginning of their relationship now fades away and subsequently becomes a source of frustration, embarrassment, fear, and pain.

There are many survivors who have lived most of their adult lives without ever consciously knowing about the abuse, yet the abuse has deeply affected their lives and their sexual relationship. I believe there are many couples who have suffered through years of emotional pain and deprivation in their sex life. The oldest survivor I ever had in counseling was 57 years old when she discovered (started remembering) the abuse. Many simply turn off to sex in any form. Survivors have related to me that whenever they wanted to make love or initiate sexual contact they felt like a whore, or guilty and bad. Some aspects of lovemaking may seem repulsive or invasive. A male survivor spoke of the change he experienced once he started remembering: "I used to enjoy oral sex too, but now it's sometimes repulsive."

For some, the unconscious emotional conflicts may get translated into physical manifestations. Men may develop impotence or prostatis. For women there seems to be a broader array of physical problems that are related to conflicts stemming from sexual abuse. In addition to those commonly accepted, such as being non-orgasmic or "frigid," it is less known that many times such things as frequent vaginal yeast infections, altered menstrual periods, unusual bleeding, vaginismus (lack of lubrication during intercourse), and tender or painful breasts, may also derive from sexual abuse.

The survivor may migrate from being " not interested," to developing a strong aversion to sex during some stages of the healing process. Some survivors may reluctantly participate in sex, but continue practicing their childhood survival techniques, such as "not being there," a way of dissociating, or going numb during intercourse. As one said: "Sometimes I'm not really there." They may distract themselves by thinking of other things, even simple things like planning meals or a shopping list, or imagining they are with someone else. They may even pretend it is not happening at all. Needless to say, this type of behavior is acutely painful for the Partner. At times he feels he might as well be making love with a zombie.

During times of intense healing activity it is common for the survivor to be less interested in sexual contact. Frequency of sexual intercourse may diminishes during early stages of healing sexual abuse. Sex may be so threatening that the couple may not make love for weeks or even months at a time. When this happens, the Partner becomes increasingly conscious of the time and distance between their lovemaking experiences. He experiences pain because he feels rejected emotionally and sexually. The pain is more acute when the change in behavior is sudden, as it was for this Partner:

> "I have come to like and enjoy sex a lot in the past few years. But my sexuality is rejected by my partner right now and it's confusing and hurts!"

Another partner lamented:

> "Why do I feel so abandoned and rejected when we can't have sex?"

Meanwhile, in the survivor's mind, the time interval between sexual experiences becomes compressed or even disappears. When confronted, the length of time since their last sexual encounter will seem like negligible, rather than three months. Some couples have related that it has been a year or more since their last lovemaking. While acknowledging the pain for the Partner, we must also remember this whole issue can be painful for the survivor too, as it is for instance when sex evokes terror. In any relationship, the longer any aspect of the relationship is avoided or put off, the more difficult it is to approach. Sex is no exception. This Partner's testimony captures another aspect of the exquisite dilemma:

> "When we are not having regular sex, the longer we go, the harder it is to ask. Sometimes I think, just wait until she asks, and I'll say no then. But then when she does, though I want to say no, I'm afraid to do that. It might be a long, long time before she is interested again."

Not only does the Partner feel the pain of the absence of sex in their relationship, but he may become increasingly fearful about approaching the survivor sexually. Fear of initiating sex may lead to greater and greater frustration. His frustration and anger, perhaps at a low level at first, can accelerate and grow, to be eventually expressed quite suddenly to the survivor. His anger may serve to further distance the couple from each other, making the objective of sexual intimacy and sexual expression even more difficult. It is not at all unusual for such a chain of events to lead to increasing distance, with one or the other beginning to seek solace in outside relationships or affairs. Eventual dissolution of the relationship may follow.

If such a chain of events occurs before the discovery or acknowledgment phase of the healing, the survivor might go through several relationships without ever understanding what is happening or why. Certainly her Partners will be equally mystified. That in turn will lead to further loss of self-esteem by the survivor. Ironically, it seems that many survivors only feel safe enough to consciously acknowledge the abuse when they are in a stable relationship. It just doesn't come up otherwise.

Almost all couples dealing with sexual abuse in their history have problems in their sex life, so don't feel that you are alone.

Disinterest in sex is often the most difficult area for the Partner to handle, and it may be the most problematic for the couple to heal. From the child's perspective, sexual abuse is mostly about power and violation of boundaries, but it is also sexual. As such, sexual abuse affects the survivor's experience of her sexuality and her primary relationship. (See Appendix 5: *"How Adult Survivors of Incest Function in a Relationship."*)

GROWING UP AGAIN SEXUALLY

As we grow from childhood to adulthood, we pass through several stages of psychosexual development. When sexual abuse occurs, normal growth progression is interrupted and the child skips many stages as she is forced into adult sexual behavior. She may become stuck at a particular stage. The process of healing may require growing again through some of these stages of normal psychosexual development. This does not mean she will necessarily take the same amount of time for each stage she originally would have taken as a child. These stages can become sharply compressed in time and space; she may pass through several stages in a few weeks or a few months. So be patient with each other. Survivors need to be patient with themselves. Most want to get it over with, to have it all be "fixed" in a brief period of time. Partners, remember that you are the husband/wife or Partner, NOT her parent. Don't parent her! As suggested earlier, be her ally, not her adversary.

GIVE THE SURVIVOR CONTROL

During the healing process, the survivor needs to feel in control of her sexual experience. That control was missing when she was a child when sexual experiences were forced upon her. Now in her adult relationship, she needs to be able to feel some control. If the Partner is the one who generally initiates sex, she may still feel out of control. One way to get through this stage is to make an agreement that will give the survivor the control of their sexual relationship for a defined period of time. During this interval the Partner agrees to not initiate sex, giving the survivor the opportunity to do all the initiation. Such an agreement may be difficult for the Partner and even for the survivor as she now takes responsibility for their sex life, but I have seen it work. Of course, if the survivor uses the agreement to avoid sex entirely, then the Partner has a right to confront that behavior. While sexual relations may not be as frequent as the Partner wishes, it can be a useful compromise. With time and healing, the sexual relationship can come back into balance, and the couple can dissolve this special agreement, with the door open for either one to initiate.

Such an agreement can take some pressure off the Partner too. He no longer has to feel it's "now or never!" If he does not feel like sexual activity when the survivor proposes it or initiates it, he can say no without fear that it will never happen again, or that the period will be so long a deprivation that he dare not forego the opportunity.

SEX: WHO INITIATES IT AND WHEN?

In the best of relationships, each person should feel free to initiate sex, to make the first "moves" that lead to sexual relations, whenever he or she feels like it. The other person should feel free to respond or not to respond at any time. As most of us well know, it doesn't always work out that way. Many other factors and considerations come into the picture. Because it has been more traditional in our culture for the male to initiate sex, men sometimes feel it is their privilege to expect response or "compliance" whenever they choose to initiate sex. Some men are so threatened when the woman initiates sex that they demand that privilege for themselves alone. How tragic for both! One Partner who did so, and got the silent, resentful compliance of his wife, was able to say, years later, that it was the biggest mistake he ever made. On the other hand, many men have confided to me that they would love to have their wives initiate sex more often. They tire of always having to be the one to begin the process. It can feel like a heavy responsibility.

Understand that, to heal, the survivor may need to stop doing anything that she doesn't want to do or feel like doing, including sex. I mentioned making a temporary contract to give her total control over the initiation of sexual activity. However, if the contract seems to read: "Only in the new moon, when it's snowing out, and the kids are away at summer camp,"[1] don't buy into it! That would be dishonest and abusive to both of you. Try eventually to work out an agreement where you both have equal freedom and equal responsibility for initiating your lovemaking. And just as important, make an agreement that each of you has the same freedom to decline to participate in sex.

You might try a change of setting, a change in the time of day, making love with the lights on or in the daylight. Such changes can reduce the threat to the survivor. Going away to a hotel, motel, or cabin, away from children and the normal routines of life can be a wonderful, freeing opportunity to infuse new life into your sexual relationship.

FLASHBACKS: WHAT THEY ARE

While most sexual abuse at its root is really about power and control more than it is about sex, it is still sexual. It involves the child in sexual experiences for which he or she is not ready. When a sexually abused child becomes an adult, engaging in adult sexual activity can bring up the past as flashbacks. Flashbacks may come as fully formed memories of what happened during childhood, with *all the old feelings*. More frequently, they will come as vague impressions, partial images, but with intense emotional reactions that seem out of proportion to the triggering stimulus. The survivor may experience the terror, the anger and the shame that were present as a child but were not safe to feel or express then.

THE MANY FACES OF FLASHBACKS

Commonly, we think of flashbacks as visual images. In reality, there are others which are more common and which may prove more disturbing or mystifying.

Emotional Flashbacks

Emotional flashbacks are probably more frequent than any other, but are often not recognized as flashbacks. They may come as sudden feelings of sadness, anxiety, confusion, or fear, etc. During healing and even before, survivors commonly feel fear. Such fear may be so intense, it causes the survivor to want to hide or search frantically for someplace "safe." She may have unexpected bouts of crying for no apparent reason. When an emotional flashback occurs for which the survivor can find no reasonable cause, it can be upsetting enough to cause her to seek treatment. In the midst of such flashbacks, survivors have been known to be diagnosed as paranoid, depressed or anxious and inappropriate treatment prescribed. While paranoia, derpession or anxiety are accurate descriptions of the emotional symptoms produced by the flashback, medications may mask the true nature of the experience. They may treat the symptoms but do nothing to discern the cause and heal it.

Sensory Flashbacks

Flashbacks may be sensory in nature, such as unusual smells or tastes (semen, urine) or touch sensations on the body, especially at night. Visual images fall into the category of sensory flashbacks. They occur as sudden or fleeting images during lovemaking or perhaps as images of dark forms in the night. Sensory flashbacks may be somatic, such as mouth sores and body rashes. I personally experienced a somatic flashback when a rash appeared across my wrists in a strange banded pattern. It presented like severe psoriasis, but treating it with the usual topical medications had no effect. There seemed to be no cure for it. About six weeks after its onset, while jogging one day, I noticed I was spontaneously twisting my wrists together, as if they were tied. Moments later I had a sudden visual flashback of my hands being tied with a band of cloth during abuse. Within two days the rash was gone and has never returned. Unusual muscle contractions may also be a somatic form of flashback, as the body attempts to spontaneously activate a defense system of some kind. Often sensation and emotions are linked together.

Behavior Flashbacks

When the survivor finds herself unconsciously engaged in a certain behavior (sometimes over and over) that is in essence a reenactment of some behavior that was an appropriate reaction at the time of the abuse, she is experiencing a behavioral flashback. Compulsive behaviors such as frequent hand washing, teeth brushing, or showering because she feels "dirty" are common. Behavioral flashbacks may occur simultaneously with emotional flashbacks.

Belief Flashbacks

Belief system flashbacks manifest as expressed beliefs about the self, relationships, the world or the environment. Beliefs such as: "The whole world stinks!" or "All men ever want is sex" or "No one will ever love me!" are definitely connected to some previous event in that person's existence. Most of our beliefs about ourselves and the world were formed before the age of six, so we are often looking at the world through the eyes of a child with our beliefs.

The flashback may not include full-blown sensory or emotional experiences (visual, feelings, or sensations). It may only be a disturbing sense of something being "wrong." The survivor may feel vaguely uneasy, or the feelings may be stronger with lots of fear, rage, or confusion, yet with no memories of anything spe-

cific. One survivor speaks of recoiling in terror and repulsion anytime her husband's foot happened to touch her at night in bed if
she was not fully awake and conscious of her present surroundings. Thankfully she can now report that with healing this unconscious response has pretty well passed, and she no longer leaps
out of bed when touched in the night.

HOW TO HANDLE FLASHBACKS

So what do you as a couple living through these things do,
you ask? First, be patient and gentle. To the Partner, I want to suggest that you do not get angry, though that may be your initial response to the flashback. The survivor didn't ask for this any more
than you did! Recognize that she is feeling emotions and other experiences left over from childhood and lacks conscious control
over them. You might compare the situation to that of a child who
wakes up in the night from a bad dream or nightmare, crying and
terrified. You would not go into the child's room and begin berat-
ing the child for being scared (at least I hope you would not). You
would instead go in and comfort that child. Recognize that you
may have a "child" with you at the moment of the flashback.
Comfort her but be cautious about touching. I remember one occasion while I was lying in bed when I was in the midst of a flashback and my wife touched me. In a flash, I turned over and was
up on my hands and knees in a fetal position, trembling in terror.
Needless to say, it surprised both of us. Though touching may be
your first spontaneous reaction in an attempt to comfort, ask permission before touching.

Talk to her!

Help her to come back to reality. If it occurs in the night, turn
on a soft light. Suggest that she open her eyes and see who you
are. Remind her she is not alone, that she is safe here. That was
then, this is now. She is not back there with her abuser. Have her

look at her hands and feet, see that she is an adult and not a child. Gently say things like: "Open your eyes. Look at me. I am *(your name)*. You are safe now. No one is going to hurt you. You are okay. It's going to be all right."

A Cold Washcloth

If she has gone numb (dissociated) or freezes and goes rigid when the flashback is intense, try gently putting a cold washcloth on the inside of her wrists or on her forehead. It forces her to feel something physically in a safer part of her body, and serves to bring her back into her body. Most important, stay present! Don't leave. You may be frustrated, impatient, irritated, but don't give up. Leaving, either emotionally or physically, will only create more fear and a feeling of rejection and unworthiness, further impeding the healing and injuring your relationship.

While it is not unusual for flashbacks to occur during sex, they can occur at any time. If you are not attuned to watching out for them, or interpreting them as flashbacks, they can be quite mystifying and disturbing, even frightening. Whether you are a survivor or a Partner of a survivor, do not let unusual behavior be summarily diagnosed as "crazy." At some deep level it makes perfect sense to the person experiencing it.

IDEAS FOR BUILDING INTIMACY

Intimacy can be an elusive quality in a partner relationship. We like to define our relationships, be they marriage, or living together, or still just dating as intimate relationships. An intimate relationship depends on more than whether you are having sex or not. Intimacy carries a quality of bonding with another human being that we long for from infancy through old age. Survivors both crave it and fear it. They fear it because in the past intimacy led to abuse. They crave it because they are human. An intimate relationship is one that has love, tenderness, and affection. The participants experience companionship, an aura of privacy, and trust of their partner. The relationship may be sexual. In fact, the best sexual relationships are also very intimate relationships. For most people, and especially for survivors, intimacy is a higher priority than sex and it also can be more fearful.

Believe it or not, you can become more intimate during this time of healing and possible sexual frustration. Look for ways to build intimacy non-sexually. Share activities you love to do such as going to movies, bike riding, hiking, swimming; investigate new recreational possibilities. For relaxation, take a bubble bath together. Spend time just touching, and do it in settings other than where you usually make love, so that it is clearly not just a foreplay move. Touch areas of the body that are less sexually charged than breasts and genitals. Above all, take time to talk to each other. In fact, *make time* to talk to each other. Share what is taking place in your mind and your heart about all aspects of your life, not just your sex life. Bring flowers or special gifts. Put notes in his/her luggage or lunch. Get some candles for your bedroom. Take spontaneous picnics.

One of the more delightful times we ever had was a picnic we had under a Ficus tree in a crowded shopping mall. We made a small private space of our own by mentally shutting out all the people walking and talking around us. We made an island of quiet and intimacy. It took little preparation or time away from our otherwise busy lives, and it was wonderful.

Sustaining that feeling of closeness or intimacy is one of the more difficult challenges of marriage or any long-term relationship. In the romantic or honeymoon stage of a relationship intimacy seems easy. But as time goes on and familiarity builds, it becomes more difficult. Then it requires intentional effort and continuing attention to maintain that quality of intimacy that is so vital to a healthy relationship. I have drawn several suggestions from participants in our workshops to share with you here. They represent a sampling of activities and attitudes that these people have found to help build intimacy.

Take Time!

There is no substitute for having time together when you have the emotional and physical capacity to respond to each other. This may mean just listening when the other needs to talk. Many find it nourishing to go out to dinner together to a place where they can talk without interruptions from children or others. It is also sometimes important to set aside problems and just talk about the good things.

In the busy lifestyle that so many lead these days, finding time to be alone together is difficult. Many couples don't take time alone until they "crash" in bed at night, when they don't have energy to give much to one another. Make time together by setting up dates. Don't use your time in bed as a time for solving problems, discussing finances, or the turmoil of sexual abuse. Talking about heavy problems or issues at night likely will disturb your rest. My wife and I have found it helpful to make a rule that we do not talk about sexual abuse, finances, or heavy decisions after 9:00 P.M.

Be the most sensitive lover you can be. To do that requires that you slow down. A quickie is wonderful when you are both in the mood and that is all the time you have. But if you seem only to have time for quickies, you will not build the kind of intimate and satisfying love life you would like to have. Recognize your needs for intimacy and touch.

It's the Little Things!

Pay attention to the little things, such as simple considerations and courtesies. Do things for each other spontaneously, such as giving a card when it is not a birthday, Valentines Day or other special occasion. Write a love note and put it in his or her lunch, or hide it in the suitcase when going away on a trip . . . just to say: "I love you."

Some people like surprises. Others don't. For survivors, surprises may be very threatening. Knowing what is going to happen is an important part of their feeling safe and being comfortable in the world. A surprise trip, when the survivor does not have opportunity to plan or prepare herself or himself, can be an enormous source of anxiety and anger. She **needs** to know what is going to happen. Surprises in childhood may have been the prelude to abuse . . . and surprises that take the survivor to strange places or unknown territory can be very threatening. Telling survivors that there is a surprise in store for them may be setting them up for times of great anxiety rather than great expectation and joy. On the other hand, surprises that are in the form of a gift or something tangible are less threatening.

Activities

Try sharing a pleasurable activity, such as hiking, camping, or being in nature together. Reading books together in bed, watching movies together, or just sitting by the fire together can build intimacy. Sharing something that comes from your own creativity, such as a poem or a drawing, is another way of letting your partner know you on a deeper level.

Time Alone

In order for two people to come together in intimacy, each must have his or her "bucket" filled. Both need to have time and energy to nurture themselves in order to give fully to another. Thus, time alone actually enhances intimacy. Take care of yourself so you don't resent giving to the other. Give your partner time alone. If you have children, offer to take total responsibility for the children so she can have time for self-nurturing. Give her space to do things that she enjoys.

Soft Touches

This topic would not be complete without offering some special suggestions to enhance your sexual intimacy. Our workshop participants have come up with many creative suggestions. First, it is important to recognize that you need to make mental and emotional contact before you make physical contact. When beginning physical contact, begin with safe touch, sensual, but non-sexual touching. This may take the form of foot or head rubs, back rubs, neck rubs, etc. Give each other a massage by candlelight, or take a bubble bath together by candlelight. Create an attractive environment for your loving. Bring music to the bedroom, perhaps with a glass of wine, if you like. Rose petals on the bed were something special for one woman. Another woman proposed a "Sexual Sonata" composed of "a beginning movement, a faster movement, a slow movement, a fast movement, and conclusions!"

When you get to the more specific sexual contact, don't forget to talk. Telling your partner what feels good and what does not is essential to good sex. Share your fantasies with each other. Be playful! Sure, sex can be serious, but don't make it too serious. Allow yourself to be playful with your bodies. Enjoy each other. Notice the pleasure of skin contact, touching your partner and allowing yourself to be touched. Give each other a "hair caress" (brush your hair over your partner's body). Allow yourselves to feel special, attractive, lusty, and joyful. Perhaps you can imagine what puppies would be like tumbling about together. Try playing like that. Offer your lover a coupon book of special treats that can be redeemed at any time, and must be honored. And last, but not least, have fun!

1. Ellen Bass & Laura Davis, *The Courage to Heal*, pg. 337.

9

WHO IS
THE
VICTIM?

∗

*"I feel helpless and like I'm not doing enough
to ease the pain. Sometimes I wonder
if I'll ever get my partner back."*
A PARTNER

Each time we convene one of our workshops, I am struck initially by how much pain there is in the room. By the end of the workshop I am equally struck by how much strength people have to triumph over their pain. The capacity of human beings to endure, struggle and grow is truly inspiring. Normally we think of the person who was abused as the victim or survivor. But the Partner suffers great pain too. In couples in which one person was abused, the Partner becomes a victim too and is forced to suffer pain with the survivor. What kind of pain?

- The pain of knowing his spouse or partner has been violated
- The pain of seeing his partner in turmoil, upset and pain month after month.
- The pain of being repeatedly rejected sexually and emotionally over long periods of time.

- The pain of his anger toward the perpetrator especially when he has to interact with him. Carrying that rage is not pleasant.
- The pain from his insecurity and anxiety about whether his relationship with the survivor will last through the healing process.

HOW THE PARTNER IS VICTIMIZED

By Keeping The Secret

Survivors tend to be very cautious about revealing their abuse to anyone. It is hard to trust others with this most tender part of one's life. Thus they are usually slow to reveal the secret. The Partner is a victim of the need for secrecy as he attempts to respect the autonomy of the survivor to tell the world or confront her family in her own time. Remember that one of the most damaging aspects of sexual abuse is the violation of boundaries. When or if to tell is one more boundary for the survivor. It is essential that the Partner convey to the survivor that he will respect her boundaries. This respect will foster the development of self-respect and confidence that she can establish and maintain her own boundaries.

However when the secret is still held, with the confrontation incomplete, it creates incredible turmoil and pain for the Partner. He is victimized in the process because he often has to continue to interact with the family members and even the perpetrator. Each time he is around the perpetrator(s) he must live with the awareness that here is the person who violated his wife or here are the people who did not protect her. He must try to keep his anger at these people suppressed. Even when he does his best to avoid being in the presence of the perpetrator, there will be occasions, such as family reunions, funerals, etc, where he cannot avoid the perpetrator or the non-protecting parent.

By Being Isolated in His Pain

Both the survivor and the Partner typically feel alone in their struggles, especially if the past abuse is still a secret. Only very recently has sexual abuse begun to be known in the media and in literature. Abuse survivors usually grow up in isolation from other people who are having similar experiences. Threats from the perpetrators to keep the abuse secret enhance this isolation. Thus, if survivors remember it at all, they may come into adulthood feeling that they are the only ones in the world to whom this experience has happened, as was true for this woman who said: "I will never forget the first time I heard the word incest and realized I wasn't the only woman with an awful past!" Their embarrassment at talking about it, coupled with the continued subtle or not-so-subtle threats from the perpetrator, inhibit them from talking about it and finding other survivors.

For the Partner the past abuse may also be a source of embarrassment. If the survivor is isolated, then the Partner is also. If he carries the erroneous perception that he is the only one with a spouse or partner who has this "problem," he doesn't talk about it with others either. He bears it alone. Typically he does not know how or where to access support for his experience or feelings.

There is presently little organized support for Partners. This was certainly true for me when I was going through the worst of the experience, which was before sexual abuse came out of the closet. Though I did have two male friends with whom I had lunch regularly, and who would listen to my feelings, I still felt lonely.

Our workshops for couples have addressed this particular need. They provided Partners, usually men, though sometimes women, with a place to find companionship and sympathetic understanding of their plight. (See Appendix 7) The workshops also provide a place for the couple to become more clearly aware of the stress inflicted on the relationship by the abuse. With this awareness, the couples can then more fully engage in healing the relationship. (You may write to us at the address in the appendix for further information on the workshops, especially if you are interested in having us offer one in your area.)

By The Survivor's Anger

Incredible anger and rage can and do emerge in the survivor during the healing process. When directed at the Partner it tends to victimize him. It generally was not safe for the survivor to feel or express the anger in childhood. Now only those closest to the survivor provide a sufficiently safe environment to express that anger. Thus the spouse, Partner, or the children of the survivor may become her innocent victims.

As the anger begins to surface, Partners sometimes become identified with the perpetrator. One partner in our workshop describes his experience like this:

> "She blames all males, me included, for what
> happened to her. It seems I must share some of
> the guilt for these crimes because I am male and
> most are committed by us!"

The survivor may project onto the Partner the least desirable characteristics of the perpetrator, lashing out with accusations such as: "You're just like my father (brother, uncle, grandfather, etc.)!" "All you want is sex. You don't care about me!" In her quest for safety, the survivor can unconsciously use her anger to distance herself from all people, including those in her primary and most important relationships. She may not even understand that anger herself and be frightened by it. As one survivor put it:

> "How am I ever going to do this work? I am so
> terrified that the anger and rage, like a monster,
> will overwhelm and destroy me."

By Emotional And Sexual Rejection

As explained in Chapter 8, the survivor frequently is not interested in sexual contact during certain parts of the healing, or is at least less interested. The Partner feels victimized by this loss. He may wonder what he has done to deserve this kind of treatment. Perhaps even more painful is the *emotional* withdrawal that accompanies the healing. Survivors are frequently preoccupied with their healing and paying attention to others and their needs seems like a distraction from what is really important at the moment. In extreme cases, when the abuse is not dealt with directly, the emotional unavailability may persist for years or become a permanent lifestyle of the survivor.

In addition, the survivor, in her quest for safety, may be constantly leaving...either emotionally, or threatening to leave physically. Such threats to leave or run, or actually breaking off the relationship, in effect victimize the Partner. He feels powerless to do anything about it.

THE VICTIM-RESCUER DILEMMA

The Partner often finds himself in a dual role. In the classic victim triangle, there are three major positions: victim, persecutor and rescuer. Usually the Partner is in the role of rescuer or supporter. But when the triangle rotates and he becomes the victim of the survivor's anger, sexual withdrawal, etc., it becomes confusing to him. He may have accepted the role of supporter/rescuer. He is then dismayed when he himself feels abused by the circumstances. He faces the dilemma of finding the most effective way to behave in this new situation. The most certain way to break the victim triangle is for the person in the victim role to refuse to play victim any longer.

One of the implications of the meaning of the term "victim" is that the harm or suffering stems from no action or fault of the victim himself. He has done nothing to precipitate it or bring it on himself. In effect he has no power over the harm. Having no power over the outcome becomes an insidiously destructive aspect of the experience. If the Partner chooses no longer to be victim, and not allow himself to be victimized by some of the aspects just described, it will shift the balance of power in the relationship, and force changes in behavior and possibly the personality of the survivor. As the Partner is working to be supportive of the survivor, the relationship sometimes becomes increasingly painful. He may not allow himself to perceive himself as being victimized. He accepts the situation as "just the way it is."

In my own case, it was only when some of my friends confronted me and asked me how much longer I was going to be a victim that I realized I was also being victimized. When put that way, I rapidly concluded that I didn't want to remain a victim. Since my particular "hot button" was around the issue of abandonment, my wife's threats to leave were the most painful for me. Though I was afraid that it would precipitate the end of our marriage, my confrontation with her was actually helpful to her in breaking the cycle of running.

The Partner walks a precarious dividing-line between being a victim and being supportive. He needs to maintain his own integrity and strength, without becoming another abuser of the survivor. In the next chapter I offer some suggestions for how the Partner can do this in the face of such a great challenge.

10

HINTS FOR COUPLES DURING THE HEALING PROCESS

*

"I don't know what to do to help."

I n the midst of the conflicts that arise during the healing process you may frequently find yourself in conflict with your companion. At these times it is easy to become adversaries. Remember, *you are in this together*. Healing is not just the survivor's job. If you can adopt the idea that you are fighting together to be well and whole, the battle will be much easier. Remember that the survivor did not create this situation. She was not responsible for the abuse happening. You each need to know that the other is going to be there for you. You need to know that you are teammates as you fight through the phases of healing. Discuss it together and work out ways you can be **allies** during this time. If you find yourself angry a lot, try directing your anger at the perpetrator rather than at each other.

MAKE THE COMMITMENT TO HEAL

The commitment to heal must be a shared one. Of course, the survivor must be the first to make this commitment, but it takes both of you. I have discovered more than one level to this commitment. In the case of my own abuse, I quickly made a mental commitment to heal. But several months later I realized that I had entered an emotional commitment to heal that went far deeper than anything I had previously known or experienced. It involved a reorganization of my life, my priorities, and my sense of self. The same thing is true in my commitment to my wife and to her healing as it continues.

Full healing requires commitment from the Partner. This may come as a surprise to you as a Partner. If you do not make this commitment as well, you may find that you are unconsciously sabotaging the healing process. You may be frustrated with how long it is taking. You may say: "Why don't you just forget it, let it stay in the past?" You may put pressure on the survivor to hurry up the healing, perhaps to spend less money on therapy. In many subtle and not so subtle ways you may be letting her know that you are not with her in this healing process. She needs you at her side, now more than ever. She needs you to stand by her, support her, and encourage her in this process. If you can give her that support, she will recover much more rapidly than if you do not.

WHAT TO DO WHEN
THE ABUSE IS STILL A SECRET

Many survivors have kept secret their childhood sexual abuse. Only recently has it been more socially acceptable to let such information be known. Not many years ago, the psychiatric community was saying that incest or sexual abuse was so rare that the average psychiatrist might see only one or two cases in a lifetime, that the incidence was only one or two per million. Now the world is acknowledging the widespread incidence of sexual abuse and incest, and rather than one or two per million the percentages are one in three women and one in five or seven men. A number of celebrities have come out into the open about their own abuse.

The most recent, as of the time of this writing, is a former Miss America, who grew up in Denver. Some people are shocked at the widespread incidence of incest (and they should be!), while others would prefer to still keep it quiet, a dark secret.

Secrecy around sexual abuse is one of the more difficult areas for a couple to work through. Survivors and Partners may differ about how to handle it. The Partner may want to tell the whole world, and especially want to confront the abuser and his/her family. The survivor may be afraid to do that. Or the roles may be reversed with the Partner being the one afraid to speak of it. Sometimes, neither one may want to talk about it.

It is important for you as a couple to come to an agreement about handling the knowledge of the abuse, handling the "secret." This is especially true when dealing with family members and at family gatherings. Try to get beyond the stage of keeping the abuse secret.

End the Secrecy

One of the most healing (and perhaps the most frightening) things you as a couple can do is to stop keeping the secret. You cannot complete your healing until you do. As long as you keep the secret, you have to keep parts of yourself in hiding from others, and perhaps even from yourselves. You may not want to broadcast it to the whole world, but make it okay to become a known fact among your family and friends. An essential element of grief work is talking about the loss. This same principle applies to healing abuse. You need to be able to talk freely about the abuse and its effects on your lives. However, each survivor must find her own time and rhythm for revealing the secret. If the Partner reveals some of the secret before the survivor is ready, she may experience one more devastating violation of her boundaries and trust. Work together on this. Continuing to keep the abuse secret creates a tremendous strain for both of you individually and for your relationship.

ESPECIALLY FOR THE PARTNER

During the process of healing the wounds of abuse the role of the Partner is not an easy one. People have a great deal of compassion for the survivor and her pain and suffering, but few realize the pain and suffering of the Partner. The Partner, usually a male, is seldom considered during the healing process. He is supposed to roll with the punches and be there as a constant support for his spouse throughout the process. But his plight is often like this man who implored: "I don't know what to do to help." Now that we are beginning to hear from more Partners, we realize that they too need support, caring and healing. Although books and guides for survivors abound, to date I have seen none for Partners. (Laura Davis' new book, *Allies in Healing,* due out in the fall of 1991, should help fill this gap) We are just now beginning to see the emergence of organized support groups for Partners. They are long overdue.

What follows are some suggestions for the Partner during various stages of the healing process. Though I speak primarily to the Partner here, I hope the survivor will read this part of the chapter too.

Don't Take It Too Personally

In a good relationship that includes a high level of intimacy, each person identifies with the other to some extent. One of the hazards that the Partner faces is feeling as if the survivor's anger, distancing, fear, and rage are really his responsibility, his "stuff." This is not surprising in that much of the rage and distancing behavior is directed at him. The Partner must learn to allow for the survivor's distortion and projections in dealing with the abuse. The rage more properly belongs to the perpetrator and to those in positions of responsibility who should have protected the survivor.

My first suggestion, and probably the most difficult to carry out, is: "Don't take it personally!" Some Partners in our workshops have acknowledged that they too feel shame and guilt about the abuse. They too want to deny it or to keep it a secret from their public. Unfortunately this makes it more difficult to be of support to the survivor. You need not feel ashamed of yourself for what happened to your partner many years ago.

You Are Not Alone

Although you may feel isolated and alone in this process, it is important for you to know that you are not alone. With so many women having been sexually abused (some recent studies show one third of all women), many Partners are going through experiences similar to yours. Perhaps even some of your friends and acquaintances are experiencing the same feelings and the same isolation. If at all possible, get the survivor's permission to talk with others about the abuse and about your experience as a Partner. Once you begin talking you will undoubtedly find other people having the same or similar experiences. In other words, build a support system for yourself. You need one. You deserve to have one. You can create one. It is time for childhood sexual abuse and its healing to come out of the closet. Talk about it at your exercise club, at your church gatherings, or at other appropriate social occasions. Without being obsessed by the topic, give yourself permission to talk about it enough to find people with similar experiences until you build a good support system for yourself. Once you have found those supportive people, use them. One of the principles of Twelve Step programs, such as Alcoholics Anonymous, is calling others for support when you are in crisis. Use this important tool for yourself.

Unfortunately, our culture has created an independence myth for men. It teaches men not to reach out. Men are the supporters. Try out the idea that this is a myth and not a truth. If you are a male, it does not mean that you should be able to handle all things by yourself. It especially does not mean that you have to cope singlehandedly with what sexual abuse does to you and your relationship. None of us has been prepared or trained for such an experience.

As you begin to reach out for support, you probably will find once again that you have to deal with your own feelings of shame. This may be a surprising insight for you, and thus will be a helpful for you. Not all Partners realize that they too feel shame about the abuse. If they do, they are likely to keep silent about it because it is embarrassing. You may have to remind yourself over and over that you have no reason for shame or embarrassment.

Besides talking to friends and building your personal support system, you may need to talk to a counselor or therapist *experienced in dealing with sexual abuse*. He or she can help you sort out the real from the unreal and clarify your wants, needs, and expectations. You may wish to join a support group or therapy group specifically for Partners. If you don't know of any, call your local social services or mental health agency to ask if they know of any such groups. Employee Assistance Programs (EAP) at your job site may also be a good referral source.

Have Fun Again!

I also want to encourage you to reinvest in yourself. Do things that you enjoy. **It is easy to make taking care of the survivor or coping with the sexual abuse your second vocation**. Frequently Partners get so focused on working through the abuse experiences in their relationships that they begin forgetting the other things that help them to be happy and maintain balance in their lives. Such things may include exercising regularly, motorcycle riding, fishing, swimming, hiking, camping, horseback riding, gardening, recreational reading, movies, or any variety of sports activities. You need to continue to nourish yourself. Give yourselves permission to nourish your relationship too. Go out on a date with your partner. Take turns planning a relaxing evening or a new weekend outing. Get away from the abuse sometimes. Go out for dinner or go dancing. Try to remember the things you did when you were first dating that you both enjoyed. Do them again!

Communicate!

In living through this time in your lives as in all others, it is crucial that you communicate effectively. Though sexual abuse is probably the hardest thing for you to talk about, do it! Sometimes survivors are very reluctant to talk about what they experienced and what they are going through right now. They feel ashamed or don't want the added vulnerability of having other people really know how bad they feel. They worry that they will bore their family members, their friends, and especially their Partners. They don't want to be rejected. Partners, not wanting to make survivors feel worse or have more pain by bringing it up, may refrain from talking about what is happening emotionally for them. Though some things may be more appropriate to share in full with your therapist, a friend, or fellow survivor or Partner, in general, you can't heal in your relationship what you don't talk about. While it is true with all relationships, that is especially true when one of you has a history of sexual abuse.

Ask For What You Need

Learn to ask for what you need, such as time off from talking about the abuse or time to talk about it more. Ask for time for being held and cuddled or for just another hug, time for a little reassurance that you are going to get through this thing together.

This was hard for me to learn. As a child I learned that I had to take care of myself emotionally. I am a prime example of the "do it yourself" school. Thus my tendency was NOT to ask for what I needed from my wife. When I was feeling anxious about our relationship surviving, I found it especially upsetting if she said no when I asked for a hug. There are times when the survivor is in so much pain that she cannot give anything at all. Eventually I could accept that it was not the end of the world when this occurred, that there would be other days when hugs would be available. But it was painful!

Besides asking for what you need, encourage the survivor to ask for what she needs. If she seems reluctant, simply ask: "What do you need from me right now?" When you do this, try to be aware of what you want to give and what you CAN give. Going beyond what you can give only aggravates the situation and becomes abusive to you. A friend of mine once told me of a principle by which he lived: "Try to accept from me what I have to give to you. But don't try to take from me what I cannot give. It will only make both you and me frustrated and disappointed."

Be Aware of Your Limitations

Closely associated with the need for communication is the need for limits. Be aware of your limitations and don't exceed them. When Partners are trying to be helpful and give support to the survivor, it is very important for them to be aware of their limits. If you as a Partner continue to try to give beyond your limits, you hurt yourself and eventually your partner. If you do not set limits you may find yourself angry or filled with resentment, leading to further alienation. Setting limits may be very difficult, particularly when she is in crisis or in great need. It is therefore vital for her to have her own support system beyond just you, her partner. Some areas for limit setting may include:

1) being available to her when she is in crisis,
2) hearing about the details of the abuse (the reverse also may be true; you may never hear about the details and may need to ask for them),
3) knowing where your "hot buttons" are. How does her abuse interface with your sensitive issues, your special needs?

One of my "hot buttons" was a fear of abandonment that I have carried with me from childhood. When my wife was needing more space or distance from me in order to feel safe, I often felt rejected and fearful of being abandoned. When she threatened to leave the relationship or declared "it just feels all wrong," I became frightened or anxious. I interpreted her statement as an appraisal of our marriage, rather than as a description of her internal emotional state at the time. I have learned to disconnect such statements from my own hot buttons, and thus can hear them from a less defensive position. I now can respond to her from a position of empathy, caring and support, rather than panic.

Relating to the Perpetrator

Each Partner must be clear about his own limits when around the perpetrator. You cannot relate cordially if you are in a constant rage at him and want to "maim and kill!" Don't be afraid to set your limits about how much you can tolerate being around the perpetrator. You have a right to your boundaries too. Pretending to be cordial would be abusive to you.

Since the survivor was once in a submissive role to the perpetrator, she may unconsciously revert to that role when around the perpetrator and continue to be emotionally abused by him. Setting limits with the perpetrator was something she was unable to do well when the abuse was happening and it may still be difficult for her. She may need your help in restructuring her contact with the perpetrator. For instance, agree to limit the amount of time you will both be in his presence and ask her to limit contact to only when you both are present. Try to work these agreements out prior to family visits. Then each of you will have a clear understanding about your policy.

You Can't Fix Her Pain

Coping with her pain, grief, and possible depression may be the most difficult task for the Partner. You may ask yourself from time to time, "How did I get into this, anyway?" It is now becoming known that sometimes Partners of abuse survivors are attracted unconsciously to survivors in order to be able to help them. I know of Partners who have divorced one survivor only to marry another woman who later becomes aware she is a survivor.

Somehow they recognize in the woman (who may not have known she was a survivor) someone who needs a supportive person. If you, the Partner, are one of those "helper" type people, you may be in for a big surprise in trying to "help" this person. It is important to realize that healing these wounds *never* involves a quick fix. While it is normal to want to heal or fix anyone who is in severe physical or emotional pain, this is one situation you can't fix! Seeing someone in pain creates discomfort for most normally empathic human beings, but you cannot take her pain away. However, you can be supportive.

Recognize that the survivor may not want your help, at least not in the way you want to give it. Rather than being "fixed," most survivors want a witness, someone who will not abandon them as they ride the emotional roller coaster of the healing journey. Helping someone often gives the helper a feeling of power or of being in control. If being in control is part of your payoff for helping this person, you are going to be given many opportunities to let go. While this no doubt will benefit you in your own long term growth, the survivor's increased strength and independence may initially create discomfort and conflict in the relationship, as positions of power shift.

Be Aware of Suicide Risks

Recognize that though the healing process may be stressful for both of you, it is especially so for the survivor. Be aware of any possible suicide risks. Suicide threats and risks usually come when a person is depressed and angry. Keep emergency telephone numbers available. Encourage the survivor to call friends and other support people when she is in crisis. If she is feeling suicidal, know whom you or she can call for counseling and support. If she is definitely suicidal, call a professional person trained to help in situations like this. Most communities have a hot-line of some kind. If she is in therapy, call her therapist.

Beyond this kind of preparation, get a "no suicide" pact. This means getting a personal commitment that no matter how bad it may get, she will not attempt suicide. Get an agreement that she will call for help instead of making an attempt on her life. Assure her that this will help her to feel *more* in control of her life. Serious suicide attempts usually will result in hospitalization (medical, psychiatric, or both) with an accompanying loss of personal autonomy and control.

What You Can Do

If you can't fix her pain and make it better overnight, what can you do? The simplest (though not necessarily the easiest) strategy is to listen, listen, listen. Then listen some more! When listening, don't just pretend to listen while you go on with your activities (reading, watching TV, eating, etc.). That doesn't work! I know because I used to try that sometimes, and it only aggravates the survivor, communicating that you aren't really interested. Don't do it! Sit down, look at the person, and give her your full attention. That is what she needs at those moments.

Help the survivor focus. Ask her what she needs from you right now, indicating that you are available to try to meet that need to the best of your ability. Don't try to ignore it, fix it or even make it better. You probably can't. Acknowledge her feelings. Acknowledge that it is okay for her to feel the way she is feeling. The feelings may be ones she has carried from childhood, which were appropriate in that childhood situation, though they may not fit today's reality. She needs the freedom to *feel* the feelings . . . the anger, the fear, the terror, the revulsion, etc., in order to get through them. Feelings, given space, will move on through and be released. All feelings are transitory.

Give extra support in simple physical ways too. Help out more around the house with the children, household chores, and food handling. Suggest that she try some of her favorite ways to relax and nurture herself, such as time to write in a journal, take a bubble bath alone (without children or husband around), or go out to lunch.

Building Trust: A Step-By-Step Process

When a child has all her boundaries violated by someone who was a trusted caretaker, it destroys much of her capacity to trust. Where she once trusted, she has learned it is not safe to trust. Though she loves you, it may take a long, long time to trust you. You can help this trust building process by being aware of her handicap, and by being as trustworthy as possible. Do you keep your commitments? Are you on time and present when you say you will be? Do you follow through with what you say you are going to do? When you are doing planning together, try to clarify her expectations as well as your own. You both have, in your own minds, some very specific expectations, so don't be verbally vague. To build trust, make those expectations explicit and then honor them. Expect her to honor them too. The survivor needs to experience herself as trustworthy. She needs to be able to trust herself. If she believes that she cannot be trusted, then she will not believe that anyone else can be trusted either.

Provide Reality Checks

A very strange distortion of reality occurs during the healing of sexual abuse. When a survivor is working through feelings repressed as a child, experiencing those feelings again is part of the healing process, but they will seem strange, because they do not fit the present-day reality. During such a flashback (see Chapter 8), the survivor has temporarily exchanged her current reality for an older historical reality. Fear is the most typical example of an emotional flashback that surfaces in this way, with anger a close second.

Since acknowledging that I too am a survivor, I sometimes have had days of feeling anxious and fearful, and occasionally terrified. Yet, in my adult mind, I cannot identify anything in my present reality that justifies those feelings. I have learned that when such feelings occur it does not mean I am going crazy. It merely means I am feeling childhood feelings that were not safe to feel then. I try to remind myself that it is safe now to feel the feelings. I recall a day not long ago when I was feeling very fearful. I didn't know whether to cry (which I did), shout, scream, or just go hide in a corner somewhere. It was such a powerful experience of feeling unsafe in the world.

At times like those just mentioned, it may be useful to remind the survivor that you are **not** the perpetrator. Say in a clear, firm, but not angry, voice: "I am **not** your (father, brother, uncle, baby sitter, mother, etc.)!" You may need to say it several times to get through to her. Remember she may be in a different reality than the one you think you are sharing. It may take a few moments to penetrate that other reality. There probably are some elements in your current situation, no matter how remote or obscure they appear to you, that remind her of that old abusive situation and spontaneously trigger the feeling.

You also can assist the survivor in returning to her current reality by not abusing her yourself. Don't bring up the abuse constantly. Don't call her "damaged goods." Don't take the easy way out and blame all her problems or your relationship problems on the abuse. If you see "the abuse" lurking around every corner and under every bush, just waiting to trip you up and cause problems, you will be more likely to blame all your problems on "the abuse," as if to say: "It's not me, it's the abuse!" Take responsibility for your own contributions to any problems you might be having.

HOW LONG WILL IT TAKE?

You may ask yourselves, "Will these wounds ever heal?" The answer to that is: "YES!" How long will it take? That, of course, is unknown and completely individual. I would anticipate that the effects of the sexual abuse will resurface from time to time throughout your life together. But its disturbing influence will be less each time it comes up. The length of time it takes for each disturbance to pass will diminish. You can hope for better times ahead. To help you assess how far along you are in your healing process, review the stages of healing in Appendix 3 and Appendix 6.

If thinking about that level of commitment seems too big a bite for you to take all at once, then "bite size" your commitment so you don't choke on it. Make a small commitment that you know you can stand behind. For example the Partner might say: "I commit myself to supporting you being in therapy for this next year. I'll help make that a priority in our budget. At the end of that year, let's sit down together and evaluate." Or even more simply, "Let me just hold you tonight, with no sexual moves or expectations." The survivor might say: I commit myself to not run away and to go see my therapist each week.

You are in this together. Acknowledge that the healing belongs to both of you now, not just the survivor. You are healing long held wounds in the survivor, and healing the current wounds to your relationship and to the Partner. A useful approach for my wife and I has been to view this healing task as we would any other major health problem for one of us or one of our children. Without blame, we both become willing to be transformed by this healing process. Without blame, we both emerge from it stronger, more loving and more whole persons. I offer this hope to you. Best wishes!

INDICATORS
OF
CHILD SEXUAL MOLESTATION
IN ADULTS

(For self evaluation, place a check mark in the blank preceding those items that match your experience.)

*1. ___ Do you experience unusual behavior during sex such as crying, panic, sudden loss of interest.

*2. ___ Do you ever have a feeling during sex of being absent, out of the body, numb, etc.

*3. ___ Do you have a superhuman ability to control your thoughts and feelings during stressful situations, life crises, or during intense emotional feelings such as closeness (loving) or vulnerability.

*4. ___ Do you have phobic reactions (far more than just not liking) to foods such as mashed potatoes, rice, custard, oatmeal, mushrooms, yogurt, etc.

*5. ___ Do you ever have a feeling of choking or strangling in the back of the throat in times of stress, crisis or while crying.

*6. ___ Do you have problems with trust, such as feeling generally mistrustful but also occasionally being too trusting and thereby harmed by others. ___ This is often accompanied by the tendency not to go to the bathroom until significant bladder discomfort develops.

*7. ___ Do you have a feeling of being unreal, distant from yourself, sometimes even a feeling of being outside your body. ___ Do you ever have a vague feeling of not belonging when you are in a group of friends or with a friend. Sometimes this takes the form of a vague sense of menace when around someone else's relatives.

8.   ___ Do you have unexplained anxiety attacks, bouts of crying or fear.

9.   ___ Do you feel anger toward or fear of the opposite sex; this is often coupled with a hesitation toward, negative feelings or baseless anger toward the same sex.

10.   ___ Do you sometimes engage in seductive behavior (flirting) with the opposite sex, not aimed at a single romantic interest, and often followed by a withdrawal from the person(s).

11.   ___ Do you experience chaos in your personal life, especially chaos that is repeated and seemingly baseless. Being a workaholic may replace or go along with the chaos.

12.   ___ Do you have intermittent or continuous feelings of distance or baseless anger toward one or more of your own children.

13.   ___ Do you have a leaning toward sexual relations outside of the home—meaning preferring sex at another location or relationships beyond a primary one.

14.   ___ Do you have a personality characterized by overdone efforts at controlling others often coupled with little evident self-control.

15.   ___ Do you experience an inability to cry; feelings seldom or never expressed spontaneously.

16.   ___ Do you experience eating disorders, consisting of either thinking about what to eat next while eating, or a dislike for food that really amounts to not wanting anything in the mouth, including food, utensils, liquids, etc.

17.   ___ Do you have a pattern of sexual relations characterized by comfort and enjoyment in the beginning, followed by conflict or disinterest later, or even repulsion in individual cases.

18.   ___ Do you have an aversion to sex, especially with a history of sexual enjoyment in earlier years. This pattern might be with one or more sexual partners over a period of time.

19.   ___ Do you have compulsive behavior patterns, (such as rigid cleaning patterns, household order, etc.). This may also include rigid religious beliefs.

20.   ___ Do you have vague physical or personal boundaries—such as an inability to maintain a comfortable distance from others. Also associated with this, persons will sometimes have very few dislikes or be willing to go along with whatever others want.

21.   ___ Do you experience sexual identity confusion (homoerotic). This is often associated with cases of child sexual assault where the assault was by a person of the same sex as the victim.

22.   ___ Do you have dreams or night terrors of being sexually assaulted? This may become more generalized to being simply physically attacked or threatened.

23.   ___ Do you experience "sexualized" thinking in which the sexual connotations or the subject of sex runs frequently through your mind. Sometimes people who have this problem do not realize it because they think everybody thinks the way they do.

Notes on the Indicators:

1. Any of the starred (*) indicators indicates a high likelihood of a history of sexual abuse. Two starred indicators with any other indicator(s) yields the highest confidence of a history of child sexual abuse. Without any starred indicator, ten or more indicators are needed to conclude sexual abuse has occurred.

2. No. 1, in a very general way, may point to specific sexual acts that were part of a child's molestation if they occur at specific times in the adult's life such as during vaginal fondling, oral sex, etc.

3. No. 13—Sexual relations outside the house, and No. 22—dreams or night terrors, are both strong indicators that sexual abuse occurred in the home. Night terrors suggest that the child was molested in the bedroom or in bed after going to sleep.

4. No. 4 & No. 5 are very strong indicators of forced oral sex at a young age. They are often present when there is no conscious memory of forced oral sex.

Used by permission of the author, John Dean, MSW
7850 Vance Drive, Ste 183, Arvada, Colorado 80003

TROUBLING MENTAL EXPERIENCES AS INDICATORS OF CHILD SEXUAL MOLESTATION

1. Recurring nightmares with manifest content of one or more of the following:

    1) Catastrophes that endanger the person or family members or both,
    2) Children being harmed or killed,
    3) Person or family members or both being chased by attackers, or
    4) Scenes of death or violence or both.

2. Recurring and unsettling intrusive obsessions that take the form of the following:

    1) Impulses to harm one's own child or
    2) A sudden feeling that one's own child is in danger or is being harmed when the child is not with the person.

3. Recurring dissociation in the form of the following:

    1) Sudden sensations that one's own child is an unrelated, total stranger or
    2) Dissociation from one's own past as if the past were the past of a total stranger.

4. Persistent phobias in the form of an intense dislike of being alone and of being in physically compromised (less defensible) situations.

5. Recurring illusions in the form of the following:

    1) The frightening feeling that there is an evil or malevolent entity in the home or

    2) The frightening feeling of being entered by an evil or a malevolent entity.

6. Recurring auditory hallucinations involving the following:

    1) Hearing a child or other person crying or calling out,

    2) Hearing "intruder" sounds (for example, footsteps, doors or windows being tampered with, breathing, objects being handled or moved), or

    3) Hearing booming sounds (for example, a dungeon door closing or an explosion).

7. Recurring visual hallucinations involving the following:

    1) Movement of objects or figures in the peripheral vision (out of the "corner of the eye"),

    2) Furtive shadows or shadowy figures seen in the home or

    3) When in bed at night, the appearance of a dark, featureless, silhouetted figure.

8. Recurring tactile hallucinations involving physical sensations that may range from a light touch to being physically pushed or thrown down.

The criterion of confidence for these indicators is high if there are seven symptoms. Any combination of five symptoms with at least one perceptual (Nos. 5–8) symptom yields high confidence. Two perceptual symptoms alone are high indicators.

Excerpted from *Detecting a History of Incest: A Predictive Syndrome* by Gerald S. Ellenson, in *Social Casework,* November 1985.

TWENTY THREE STAGES OF GROWTH FOR SURVIVORS OF INCEST

1. I acknowledge that something terrible happened when I was little. I know it is not my imagination. I am aware on some level that something was done *to me*. I was a victim of incest or sexual abuse during my childhood.

2. I acknowledge I cannot manage my pain alone and seek help.

3. I begin to recognize my feelings. There may be sadness, anger, fear, guilt, and shame. I allow myself to experience them all.

4. I recognize that I am, in fact, *a survivor,* in the sense that I am *alive*, and have chosen *life* over self-inflicted death.

5. I discuss the abuse thoroughly with a therapist. I *completely re-experience* and begin to deal with feelings appropriate for *each incident* of abuse that I can recall. If I am in a survivor's group I share any feelings of shame I have.

6. I recognize and feel my anger about being used and abused.

7. I experience anger at my non-protecting parent (usually mother).

8. I tell a non-family member about the abuse.

9. I tell a family member who previously did not know.

10. I begin to recognize that I was probably acting *appropriately* at the time of the abuse occurred. (That is, my reactions were appropriate. The abuse was not!) I begin to give up my *sense of responsibility* for the abuse occurring.

11. I recognize and begin to deal with feelings of being "contaminated" or "damaged".

12. If there was a part of the molestation that was sexually pleasurable to me, I am coming to terms with the fact of that pleasure and am dealing with the guilt surrounding it.

13. If there were aspects of the molestation that I perceived as positive, (such as a feeling of being special in the family) I am beginning to understand and deal with these feelings.

14. I perceive the connection between my molestation and my current behavioral patterns and relationships. I am beginning to develop some *control* over that connection.

15. I recognize that I have a *choice* as to whether or not I *confront* my perpetrator(s).

16. I am beginning to understand what I desire from relationships, whether sexual or non sexual, as I learn to trust my perceptions.

17. I am able to enjoy intimacy.

18. I develop a sense of self and my self-esteem has increased.

19. My resistance to talking about the abuse (although not necessarily the details of it) has diminished. I can listen to the molestation of others.

20. I develop a sense of being somewhat at ease with the subject of my molestation and that of others.

21. I recognize that I have a *choice* as to whether or not I *forgive* my perpetrator(s). I *have* forgiven *myself.*

22. I am in touch with past anger, but detached from it enough so that it is not a constant part of my feelings and a negative influence on my other feelings, my functioning, and my relationships with others.

23. I live in the present and welcome the future with all its fears, imperfections, and unpredictabilities.

by Karen Lison, M.A.,
Used by permission of the author

FLASHBACKS
AND
POST TRAUMATIC STRESS DISORDER
(PTSD)

Flashbacks are not limited to visual images, but may come in many different varieties. Flashbacks are experienced in most all cases of Post Traumatic Stress Disorder. Most all people experience some trauma at some time in their life that qualifies for PTSD. No one is immune to it. It is probably the most common psychological disorder in America, though it may not be recognized as such. Following are descriptions of some of the varieties of flashbacks.

I. THOUGHT SYSTEM FLASHBACKS
    A persistent thought pattern, such as "I can never succeed, "No one likes me," is probably connected to some previous traumatic event in that person's experience.

II. FEELING SYSTEM FLASHBACKS: TWO SUBSETS:

    A. *Emotional flashbacks:*
    Overwhelming feelings of sadness, confusion, or fears that don't seem to be tied to any particular current life event (such as a death of a loved one). That feeling is very often a flashback. Examples: going to a party and feeling frightened for no real reason; having days where you feel frightened and just want to hide to feel safe. Such feelings are likely connected to some previous event in your life.

    B. *Sensory Flashbacks:*
    Smell, taste, sound, touch, imagery. These might take other somatic forms such as a knotted stomach, rashes on body

parts, strange, severe muscular contractions, or waking in the night with the sensation of having been touched. Often sensation and emotion are linked together. In the latter example, the touch would probably be accompanied by fear. Flashbacks of images, mental pictures, are actually less common than emotional flashbacks.

III. BEHAVIORAL SYSTEM FLASHBACKS
The person performs a certain behavior that is in essence a re-enactment of some previously appropriate behavior. He performs the behavior over and over where it does not apply, ie. getting angry, or patterns in relationships (come close, go away), phobias, or other compulsive behaviors such as repeated hand washing, house cleaning, bathing, etc.

IV. BELIEF SYSTEM FLASHBACKS:
Beliefs such as: "The whole world sucks." They may be beliefs about the self, about relationships, the world or the environment. It is usually connected to some past event.

Most of our beliefs about ourselves are formed before the age of six. Thus we may be thought of as looking at the world through the eyes of a child. Beliefs are sometimes connected to a thought flashback.

V. REGARDING THE DIAGNOSIS OF PTSD:
All of us are potentially subject to some minimal flashbacks from some trauma in this life, but it does interfere with our life? The following symptoms of Post Traumatic Stress Disorder (PTSD) are drawn from the DSM IIIR. Most of these occur in the lives of incest survivors. Notice whether you have experienced any of the following symptoms.

1. Recurrent and intrusive distressing recollections of the event (flashbacks). Sudden acting or feeling as if the traumatic event were recurring.

2. Numbing of affect. e.g. flat affect, and dissociation. With dissociation, you are "not here." You are in the future or in the past, or have simply gone numb. Children have been known to dissociate 90% of the time. Children who are healthy and present are so "here" that there is no mistaking them.
3. Recurrent distressing dreams of the traumatizing event or experiences similar to the event.
4. Somatic experiences such as described above in II B.
5. Hypervigilance is very common among survivors. They don't like surprises.
6. Irritability or outbursts of anger
7. Intense psychological distress (anxiety, depression, etc.) at exposure to events similar to the trauma (sexual abuse),including anniversaries of the trauma.
8. Amnesia about the trauma.
9. Sleep disturbances, including difficulty falling or staying asleep.
10. Exaggerated startle response.

VI. HELPING PEOPLE HANDLE FLASHBACKS

1. Grounding Techniques:

a) If the FB is very intense, putting cold water on the inside of the wrists helps. It forces them to feel something physically, and brings them back into their body.

b) Talk to them. "You are here in (*name the place*)." Remind them they are not alone, and of the current reality. That was then and this is now. Have them look at the calendar, and look at your hands and feet. The idea is not so much to get rid of the flashback, but to get enough distance to be able to go ahead and function.

c) Screen Technique: Imagine having a remote control device (like TV or VCR control) and with it you can turn up or down the sensations, the picture, the sound, take the color out of it, etc.

d) Use of Touch: Do this only after preparation. If you don't prepare the person for touch, it can intensify the flashback. Prepare them for the kind of touch you intend to make.

e) Use of Sound or Color: Use a "balloon" to contain it.

2. Containment Procedures

Containment means helping the client or person create some boundaries around the flashback experiences, slowing things down enough to enable the person to get through the episode and work on it later. One way to think of the flashback is to see it as "regression" work. See it as evidence that the person is now able to handle the intensity of the experience that they were not able to handle when it originally happened, even though it may still be very painful and also confusing. Following are some suggestions for "containers" and containing. The "container," into which they put the flashback, provides an arena of safety in which the person may continue to explore the experience and the trauma.

a) **Build a container in your mind.** Ask the person to design the container . . as to shape, materials, lids, doors, locks, latches, etc. Make it quite detailed.

b) **Plan where the container will go.** Know where it's going. It is not a toxic dump to bury forever. It is just a place to store the flashback experiences until you can work on them at another time. Tell them they can choose the time and place to access them. "You can have access at the appropriate time when it is safe."

c) **Containers need to be outside your body.** This is safer than having them inside.

d) **Create personal words, signals or cues to access the container or flashback.** Example: Put your hand in your pocket. Put a picture frame around the flashback. Then make a still life, and hang it on a wall or other safe place. A key is a common way of accessing. For the computer buff imagine putting all in a computer "file" and storing it away on a disk.

e) **Only the client has access to the container.** The client decides when to take something out of the container. She may only take out part of the contents, eg. the sound, or just the images, or just the fear, or just the anger, etc.

f) **Give the flashback shape, size, color, temperature, rigidity, etc.** A therapist, partner, or friend can ask continuing detailed questions of the client to assist her in describing it. It is a way of getting the client to use her mind to get hold of the flashback. This is harder to do with emotional flashbacks, and therefore sometimes you have to go to the remote control technique (see Screen Technique, No. VI, 1, c above).

HOW
ADULT SURVIVORS
OF INCEST
FUNCTION IN A RELATIONSHIP

1. They tend to move into and out of relationships quickly. This may occur as a series of fairly short term relationships. They may move in and out of houses, apartments, or other living quarters. They may develop "long distance" relationships which are very intimate and sexual, where the partner lives at some distance from them, and is thus "safe."

2. They may feel panicky, fearful when in crowded or tight places, either alone or with their partner.

3. They want close, intimate relationships, but when they get such a relationship and it becomes emotionally intimate they may push it away. They can be sexually intimate easier than they can be emotionally intimate. When the relationship begins to feel like "home," or comfortable, they run, or leave the relationship.

4. They have frequent swings of mood or emotional states, including: rage, grief, terror, crying episodes, depression, and shame.

5. In their sexual relations:
   a) They tend to become sexual easily and early in a relationship. Then they may later "lose interest." This same pattern may be played out in a shorter time frame: they behave quite seductively, engage in sexual activity and then lose interest, or turn off as soon as their partner is responding.

They may even "freeze up" when their partner responds, and act quite surprised and confused that the partner should do so.

b) They dissociate (go numb, leave their body, don't feel).

c) They have flashbacks (to former abuse scenes) and then withdraw emotionally or psychologically.

d) If female, they may be non-orgasmic, or sexually "dead". If male, they may be impotent. It is a way of not giving the perpetrator control. "I won't respond, and he/she can't make me."

6. They may become either very dependent (please take care of me and protect me) or very independent (keep your distance so I can feel safe), or they may be very controlling in the relationship (again, to feel safe).

7. There is a strong impulse to be SAFE at all costs. Being hypervigilant (constantly on guard, on the watch) is a common characteristic. This behavior can appear similar to paranoia, but is really not.

8. They may have surprising and even inappropriate reactions (such as fear, rage or extreme compliance and subservience) to:
a) certain members of their family (especially perpetrators)

b) all persons of the same sex as their perpetrators.

9. They may have difficult and sometimes inappropriate reactions to their own children. Example: A mother has sudden fears when she has to change her little boy's diapers. She fears abusing him and is confused about what would be abusive and what would not. They may have extreme rage at a child that is way out of proportion to the precipitating incident. eg: Excessive need to keep the child quiet (comes from fear related to

being noticed; as child, being noticed may have been the prelude to being abused again).

10. They find it difficult to play or enter into playful activities. Along with this they may become compulsive workers. They often have an excessive need to prove themselves (self-worth and esteem are big issues).

11. Personal boundaries tend to become easily confused, unclear or vague. They may feel frequently intruded upon, yet unable to establish or maintain personal boundaries with an intimate partner, other family members, co-workers, or bosses.

12. They tend to have disturbed or erratic sleep patterns. These may include sleep onset insomnia, being awake in the middle of the night, or have frequent night terrors.

13. Making a home is difficult. (When a domicile begins to feel like "home" it becomes dangerous. This is especially true if the childhood sexual abuse took place in the home. See Chapter 4.). This may be played out in: frequent re-arrangement of furniture; selling, giving away and purchasing new furniture frequently; frequent moves from one place to another; difficulty in spending much time at home (they are always on the move). About the time the survivor has the home arranged or fixed up according to her desire, it suddenly begins to feel "bad," or "all wrong" and she feels compelled to change it.

14. Work or behavior patterns may be compulsive:
    a) A compulsive worker . . . at work or at home. Must constantly be doing something. Never able to be still or at rest. This portrays a great need to get approval, and/or to get love and acceptance, to feel valuable and worthwhile.
    b) Work behavior may be quite erratic; is sometimes a very good, very hard worker, and sometimes a very bad worker.

    c) May move rapidly from job to job; hard to stick with any one thing.

    d) May exhibit other compulsive behaviors in areas such as eating, sex, personal cleanliness, or others.

15. Clothing and dress:

    a) The survivor may find it hard to buy clothing for him/herself, unless it is the "end of the season, last chance, bargain basement sale rack," with poor selection of size, color, etc. Underwear is especially hard to buy...unless it is something like K-Mart's cheapest.

    b) Dressing up, going out, and "being seen" is hard. (Unconsciously it may feel dangerous) They would rather fade into the woodwork.

    c) They usually have low self esteem, and low esteem of their body, and thus would rather *hide* their body than show it off. They may act this out by becoming overweight or fat.

HOW
STAGES OF HEALING
AFFECT RELATIONSHIPS

I. THE VICTIM STAGE

A. Pre-Discovery

1. Running away behaviors: ending relationships, threats to end the relationship, etc. (See Chapter 5)
2. Flashbacks: feelings, images, sensations
3. Emotional upsets, mood swings, etc.
4. Chaos in the life of the individual and in the relationship
5. Troubled sexual relationships
6. Troubled relationships with parents/siblings/family
7. Survivor dissociation, numbing, memory blocks (to parts of childhood)
8. Survivor often taken advantage of in life; may show co-dependent behaviors.

B. Early Awareness

1. Aware that something is wrong, something terrible happened in childhood
2. Angry, anxious, depressed, irritable, unsatisfied
3. Fights with partner
4. DENIAL of any possibility of sexual abuse.

C. Discovery

1. Shock, horror, distress, more anxiety, anger, etc.
2. Survivor oscillates in and out of denial that anything happened, leading to confusion for the partner and in the relationship
3. Recall of specific experiences of sexual abuse, or fuzzy memories

4. Flashbacks, (sensory, memory, etc) (See Appendix 4) with subsequent loss of feeling of safety. Survivor becomes hypervigilant.
5. Embarrassment, shame, guilt arise
6. Awareness that the secret can never be put back in Pandora's box
7. Some withdrawal from partner
8. Disturbance in relationship with partner; may be threats to end the relationship, to separate, or divorce
9. Partner feels confused, angry at perpetrator.

II. THE SURVIVOR STAGE

A. The Commitment To Heal

1. Must be made by both the Survivor and the Partner
2. Healing is made a priority in their personal and family life (and budget)
3. Usually some therapeutic process engaged: individual or group therapy for the survivor, and perhaps marriage counseling for the couple.

B. Riding the Roller Coaster

1. The feelings of both partners in the relationship are up and down, and are like a roller coaster for both persons
2. Dealing with the intense feelings (fear, anger, grief, guilt, shame) that had their origin in childhood, but are being felt now in adult life.
3. Flashbacks may intensify, and perhaps especially in the sexual relationship
4. Dissociation may occur, in the same form or a variation of the form used in childhood.
5. Grieving the loss of childhood; possible regression to child like reactions and behaviors, with consequent disruptions in primary relationship

C. The Relationship Changes

1. Basis for the relationship shifts (eg. from victim-caretaker to two strong persons). Caretaker gets "fired," is no longer needed.
2. Survivor changes primary identity: loss and renewal of (search for) identity.
3. Individual growth: death and rebirth
4. The old relationship, in effect, "dies."

D. Revealing the "Secret" and Confrontation of the Perpetrator/Misuser,

1. Decision to end the "secret" with friends, relatives, community. Survivor tells others what happened, and partner can talk about it too.
2. Confrontation seen as an option, not a necessity.
3. Method of confrontation carefully considered; implications carefully discussed both with therapist and with partner.
4. Partner support and commitment enlisted.
5. Confrontation occurs.
6. Work with family relationships after the confrontation.

III. THE THRIVER STAGE

A. Individual changes for the Survivor

1. Loss of secondary gains from compensating survival behaviors
2. Pursuit of new education, job, life goals, with resulting changes in family life
3. Re-organization of the self, identity
4. More interest in sexuality and sexual expression

B. The Relationship Changes

1. A new relationship must be built on the now current foundation of the needs and strengths of both parties.

Requires a conscious commitment to a new relationship.

2. Roles shift:
   a) The Rescuer is no longer needed (rescuers require a victim to rescue!).
   b) Survivor can take care of herself.

3. Climate in the relationship becomes calmer. Roller-coaster effect diminishes to normal ups and downs; flashbacks diminish both in number and intensity.

4. Sexual aspect of the relationship becomes more fulfilling for both. Both can initiate and enjoy it more.

5. Life takes on a fuller, richer expression. Family unit continues to grow and develop, both as a unit, and individuals in it.

HEALING THE WOUNDS
OF SEXUAL ABUSE

FOR COUPLES OR PERSONS IN A RELATIONSHIP

Who Should Come

❑ Those **ABUSED** or who suspect physical or sexual abuse as a child or adolescent.

❑ Those who are **PARTNERS IN A RELATIONSHIP** with an abused person.

❑ **PROFESSIONALS** who work with individuals in either category above.

When people who were abused (sexually or physically) as children enter a significant relationship, certain dynamics begin to emerge that are mystifying and confusing to both parties. These dynamics are often destructive to the relationship and the persons in it. **Sometimes this is the result of unsuspected abuse that is not remembered.**

Many healing opportunities have been offered to survivors of abuse but little help has been available for the relationships in which they live **or for the partners** who share their lives. This workshop addresses that gap. Using a psycho-educational model, the presenters offer practical tools for increasing awareness of the impact of childhood abuse on a relationship. The presenters will share their own personal experience in the roles of the "abused" and the "partner of the abused," in ways that offer hope and humor.

We prefer you come as couples but you may come as an individual.

TOPICS TO BE COVERED INCLUDE:

❑ How an adult abused as a child functions in an intimate relationship

❑ How the non-abused **partner** can cope more effectively

❑ How both partners can handle anger and grief together

❑ How to develop new strategies for safety and intimacy

PRESENTERS:

Mimi Farrelly, M.A. ATR. An Art Psychotherapist in private practice in Longmont, CO, and an instructor of Art Therapy at the University of Colo. at Denver. Mimi's creative approaches to healing help adult and child survivors of sexual abuse.

Paul Hansen, Ph.D. A Psychotherapist in private practice in Longmont and Denver, working with adult survivors of sexual & physical abuse. Paul uses Regression Therapy to help survivors recall memories. Paul and Mimi have been creating their relationship for 13 years and married for 11 years.

TIME: Friday evening 7–9:30, Saturday 9–4:30 (bring a lunch)

If you have questions about the workshop or want to discuss offering one in your area, please call us at (303) 652-2450.

BIBLIOGRAPHY

✳

On Incest and the Recovery From Incest

Armstrong, L., *Kiss Daddy Goodnight: A Speakout on Incest.* Pocket Books, NY 1979.

Bass, Ellen, Davis, L., *The Courage to Heal: A guide for women survivors of child sexual abuse.* NY: Harper & Row, 1988.

Bass, Ellen, *I Never Told Anyone*, NY: Harper & Row, 1093.

Bass, Ellen, *Adults Molested As Children.* Orwell, VT: Safer Society Press, 1988.

Blume, E. Sue, *Secret Survivors, Uncovering Incest and Its Aftereffects in Women,* NY: John Wiley & Sons, 1990.

Brady, K., *Father's Day: A True Story of Incest.* NY: Seaview Press, 1979.

Butler, S., *Conspiracy of Silence: The Trauma of Incest*, NY: Bantam, 1978

Caruso, B., *The Impact of Incest.* Center City, MN: Compcare Pubs., 1987

Davis, Laura, *The Courage To Heal Workbook.*

Davis, Laura, *Allies in Healing*, Harper & Row, 1991.

Engel, B., *The Right to Innocence: Healing the Trauma of Childhood Sexual Abuse,* L.A., Tarcher, 1989

Fisher, Bruce, *When Your Relationship Ends,* Boulder, CO: Family Relations Learning Center, 1978.

—— *Rebuilding.* San Luis Obispo, CA: Impact Publishers, 1981.

Gallagher, V., *Speaking Out, Fighting Back,* Seattle,WA: Madrona Pubs., 1985.

Gil, E., *Outgrowing the Pain*, San Francisco, Launch Press, 1983.

Hendricks, G., *Centering and the Art of Intimacy* Englewood Cliffs, NJ: Prentice Hall, 1985.

Hendricks, G., *Learning to Love Yourself,* 1982.

Lew, Mike, *Victims No Longer, Men Recovering from Incest*, NY: Nevraumont Pub Co., 1989.

Maltz, W., *Incest and Sexuality: A Guide to Understanding and Healing.* Lexington, MA: Lexington, Books, 1987.

Sisk, S. L., *Inside Scars,* Gainsville, FL: Pandora Press, 1987.

Warren, N., *Make Anger Your Ally,* Garden City, NY: Doubleday, 1985.

Whitfield, C. L., *Healing the Child Within; Discovery and Recovery for Adult Children of Dysfunctional Family.* Deerfield Beach, FL: Health Communications, Inc., 1987.